SKETCH: HOUSES

How Architects Conceive Residential Architecture

SKETCH: HOUSES

How Architects Conceive Residential Architecture

LOFT

Editor and texts: Alejandro Bahamón

Art director: Mireia Casanovas Soley

Graphic Design and Layout: Oriol Serra Juncosa

Translation: Jay Noden

Editorial project:

2006 © **LOFT Publications**
Via Laietana 32, 4.º Of. 92
08003 Barcelona, Spain
Tel.: +34 932 688 088
Fax: +34 932 687 073
loft@loftpublications.com
www.loftpublications.com

ISBN 10: 84-95832-63-1
ISBN 13: 978-84-95832-63-4

Printed in China

Introduction

■ Graphic representation is the most fundamental instrument used by architects in the design of a project. Nowadays, as well as traditional methods such as sketches, drawings, diagrams or plans, there are other tools used to improve how architecture is represented visually or which generate new points of view with respect to this representation, such as the digital models or photomontages. Analysing an architectural project through drawings can reveal a host of details that cannot be reflected in the construction work itself, namely, the history of the place, mechanisms used to approach the design or structural solutions. Drawings can reflect the character of the author, his points of reference, his personality and even his mood. We can also consider sketches to be works of art in themselves, in terms of composition, colour or texture.

The house is a truly classic architectural project. This building is as old as man himself, it is inherent to all societies and it shows how the model of people's private lives has evolved. The contemporary architect has, at his disposal, sophisticated technology and new materials to resolve each case depending on the needs of the client or the conditions of the site. The result is the achievement of a wide variety of typologies, such as houses between dividing walls, or the courtyard house, which architects expertly resolve.

This volume constitutes a detailed compendium of the diverse and varied graphic representations of 30 single family houses, designed by internationally renowned architects. Each one allows the reader to understand the initial inspiration for the ideas, the formal and functional development of the project, and the final details that the structure and its construction may have needed. The drawings also allow us to appreciate the different techniques used by architects today to express their ideas concerning the house.

■ Due to the reduced proportions of the site, it proved impossible to create an expressive composition that would develop on the ground. This house therefore came up with a vertical, balanced articulation on all the façades. This was achieved through a combination of fibre cement panels, a common material, and glass, which has different appearances: transparent, opaque and coloured. A concise plan was elaborated as to how to manipulate the surface, since the building, in this case, is defined more for its finish than for its volumes.

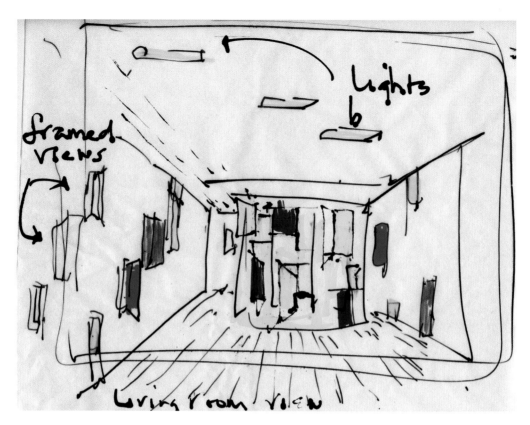

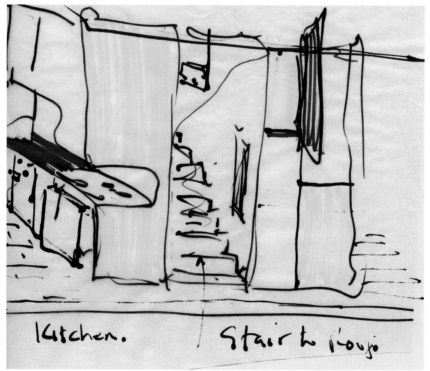

Preliminary sketches

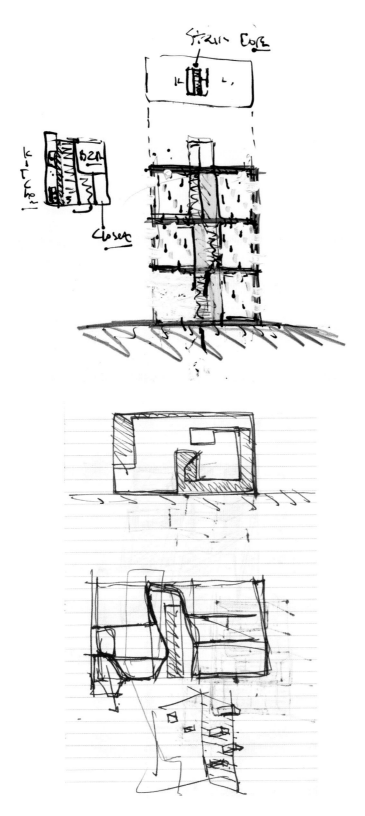

Preliminary sketches

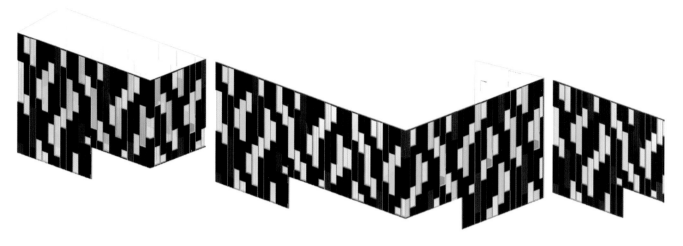

Elevations diagram

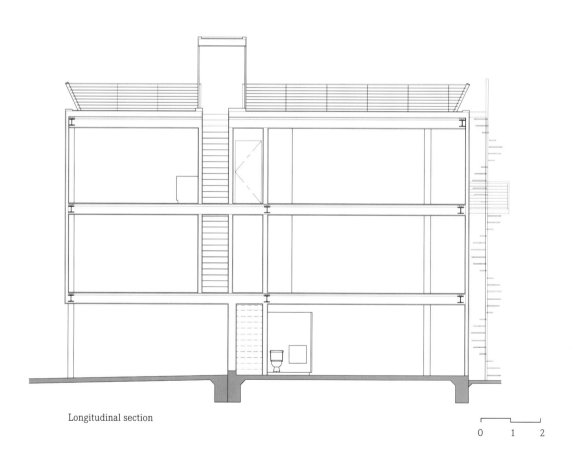

Longitudinal section

0 1 2

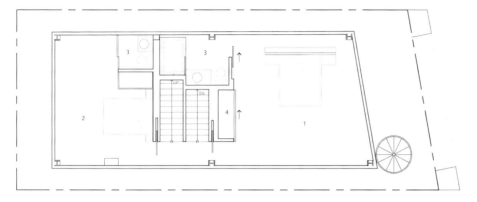

First floor

■ This work of Lorcan O'Herlihy Architects, whose headquarters are situated in California in Culver City, stands out for the refined use of the materials, the methods of assembly and an obsessive attention to the smallest of details. Permanent research, focused on the search for new materials and manufacturing methods, allowed this team to question and resolve the intrinsic relation that exists between material and design. Although they recognize the influence of modern architects such as Loos, Gropius or Neutra, they attempt to find solutions that adapt to the project's environment.

Lorcan O'Herlihy Architects

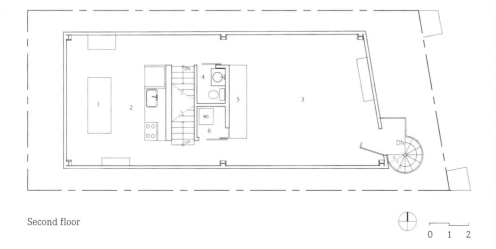

Second floor

0   1   2

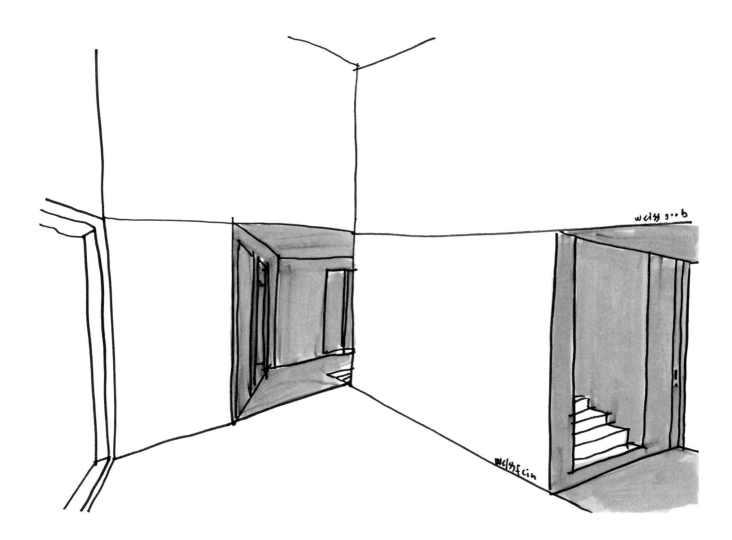

Budget: $ 1,900,000

■ This construction's distinctive form is owed to the need to take full advantage of the volume's layout, strictly marked out by town planning regulations, and thereby maximising the interior space. The general program requested by the client is resolved through a sequential plan, in which all the rooms are linked and each serves as an entranceway to the next. However each room has its own character, depending on its form, the materials used or its colour. The double-height entrance hall and library, characterised by its elliptic form, or the loggia, painted in pink, illustrate this trait. In the library, the façade is a glass mirror, which allows us to discover the garden hidden behind the books.

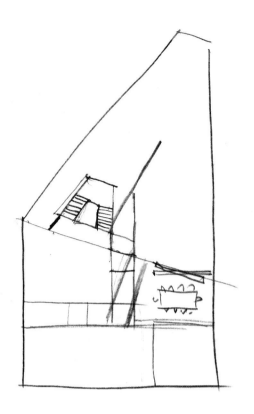

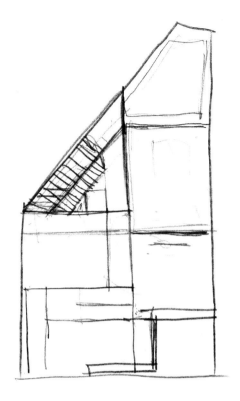

Preliminary sketches

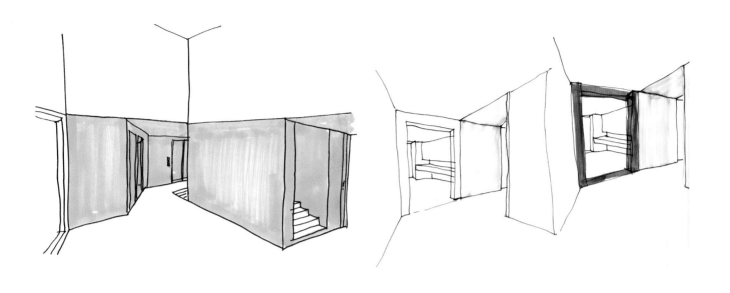

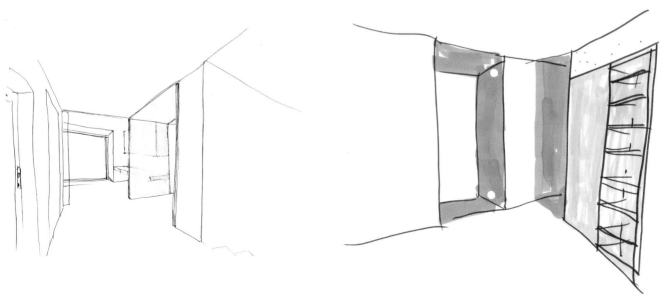

Interior perspectives

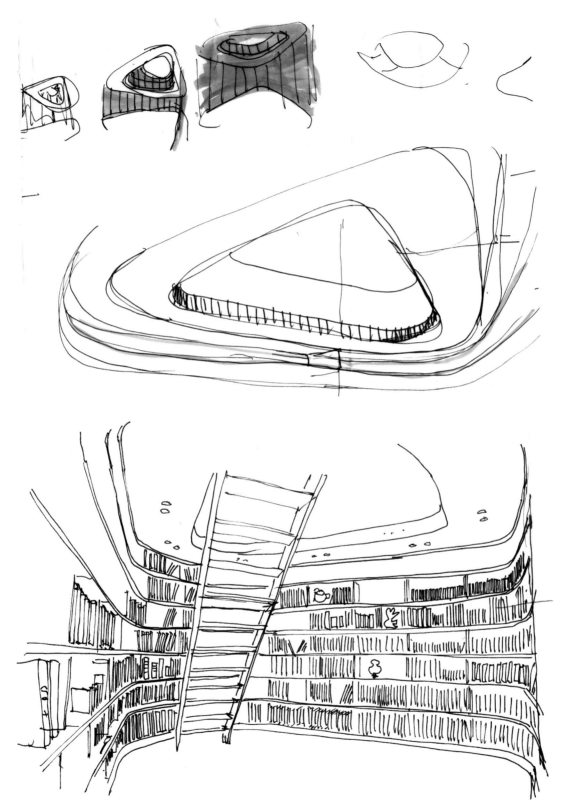

Interior perspectives

Ground floor

First floor

Second floor

0   2   4

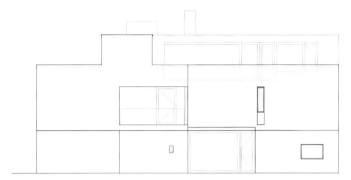

North elevation

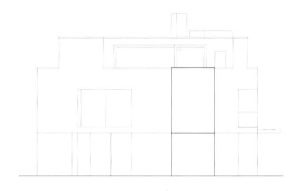

East elevation

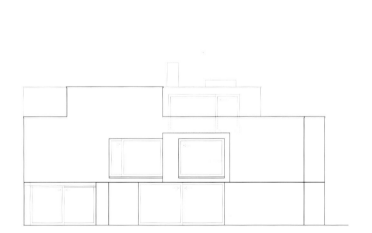

South elevation

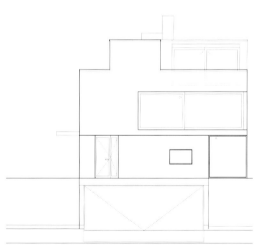

West elevation

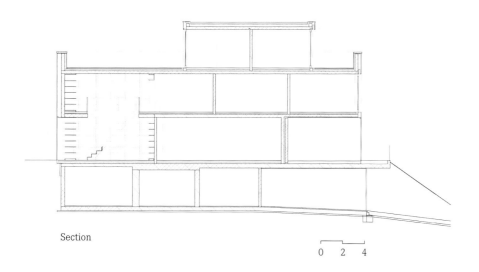

Section

```
0   2   4
```

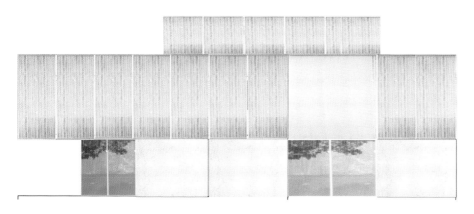

Render

■ Philippe Stuebi was born in Lausanne (Switzerland) in 1963 and graduated in architecture in Zürich in 1993. He worked for various architectural firms in Bern until 1995, when he established his own company, from where he has developed a wide variety of projects of different scales. His work has been influenced by his interest in contemporary art. Between 1989 and 1993 together with This Dormann, Thomas Wachter and Martin Frei he founded and directed, the gallery Kunstclub HeiQuell in Zürich.

Philippe Stuebi
Architekten

21

Alberto Campo Baeza **Asencio House** Cádiz, Spain

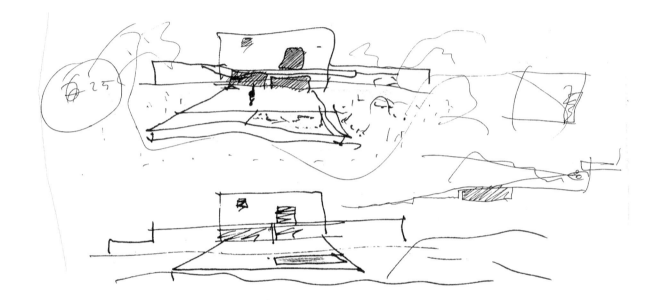

Budget: $ 329,000

■ The intense light of Cádiz, in the south of Spain, determined the design of this single family house. A composition of volumes, with obvious allusion to the vernacular architecture of Andalusia, forms a house which the light penetrates diagonally, is filtered and generates a relaxed atmosphere, the unifying element of the project. The different levels in the house emphasize where the light enters and create spaces inside with a theatrical air. The square plan has two clearly distinct areas; one facing the landscape where the living areas are located, and another facing the city, which houses the private and circulation areas.

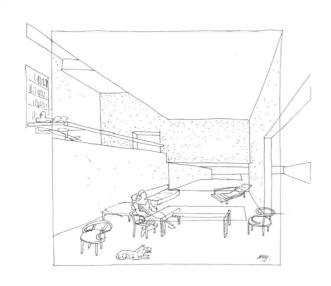
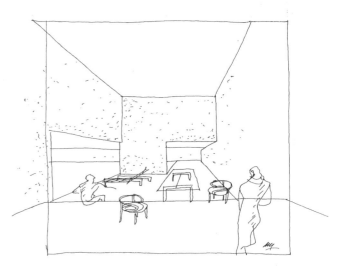

Interior perspectives

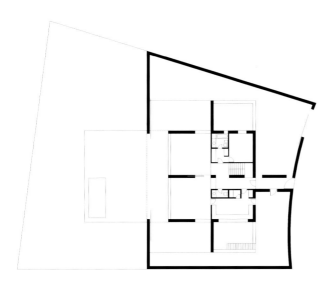

Ground floor

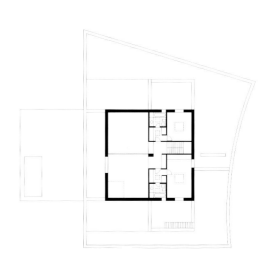

First floor

0 2 4

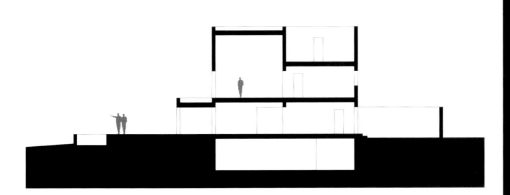

Transversal section

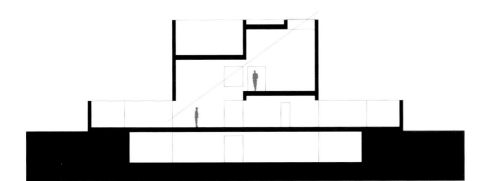

Longitudinal section

0   2   4

■ Since the beginning of his professional career Alberto Campo Baeza has combined academic tasks with the practice of architecture. His pedagogical work has lead him to giving classes in the universities of Pennsylvania, Weimar, Columbia, Vicenza and Chicago, among others. His work in the construction of well-renowned buildings such as the central offices of the Bank of Granada or those of the Editorial SM, and houses like De Blas o De Gaspar, have earned him a variety of internationally and nationally recognised awards.

Alberto Campo Baeza

Budget: $ 420,000

■ This building, as well as being a house, plays host to a private art gallery and is situated on the south-east slopes of Mount Yatsugatake, at an altitude of 4,265 ft above sea level, in the middle of a dense conifer forest. The natural slope of the plot, whose level differs by 13.12 ft from the east side to the west, as well as a constant wind, determined the typology of the project. The design is based on four curved lines that the architect drew in his sketchpad, without having any documentation for the site, except his memory from a single visit.

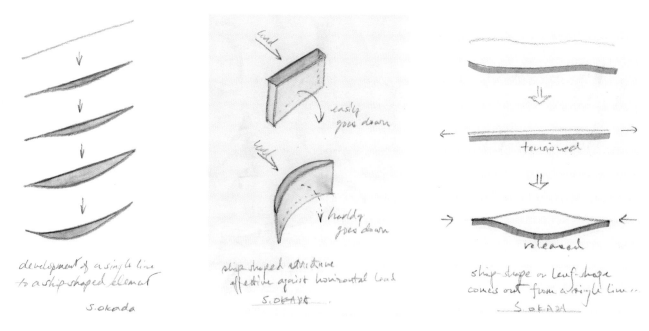

development of a single line
to a ship-shaped element

S. Okada

ship-shaped structure
effective against horizontal load

S. OKADA

ship-shape or leaf-shape
comes out from a single line...

S. OKADA

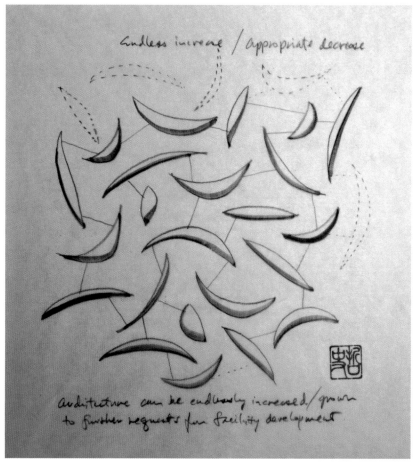

Endless increase / Appropriate decrease

architecture can be endlessly increased/grown
to further segments for facility development

Form studies

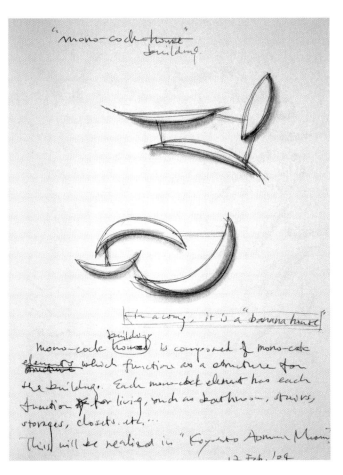

"mono-cock-house"
building.

In a way, it's a "banana house"

building
Mono-cock house is composed of mono-cock
elements which function as a structure for
the building. Each mono-cock element has each
function for living, such as bathroom, stairs,
storages, closets. etc....
This will be realized in "Koganto Annex Mnum"
                                    12 Feb. '04

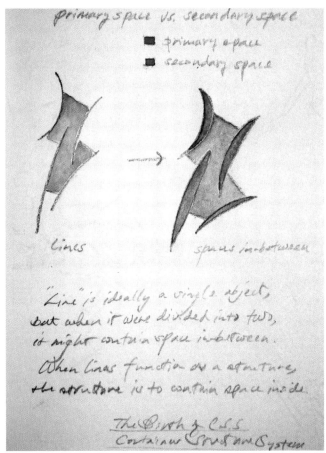

primary space vs. secondary space
    ■ primary space
    ■ secondary space

lines   spaces in between

"Line" is ideally a single object,
but when it were divided into two,
it might contain space in between.

When lines function as a structure,
the structure is to contain space inside.

The Birth of C.S.S
Container Structure System

Form studies

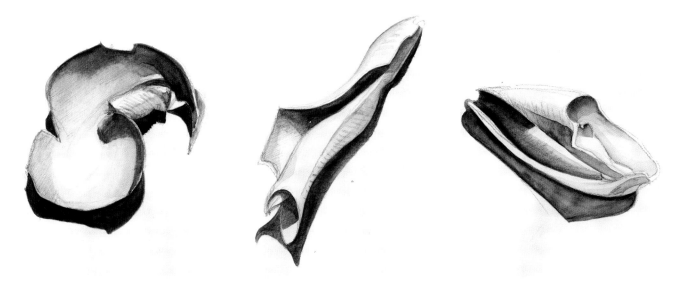

Preliminary sketches

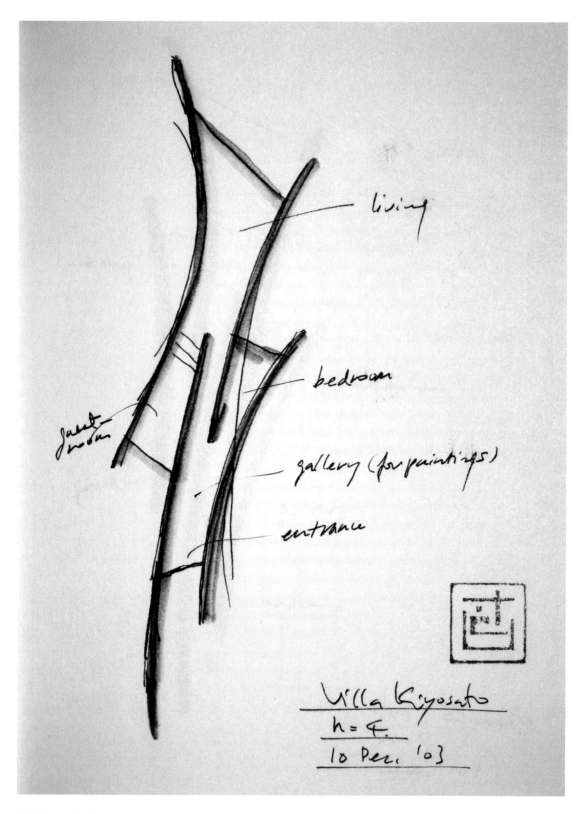

living

bedroom

gallery (for paintings)

entrance

Villa Kiyosato
h = f.
10 Dec. '03

Preliminary sketch

Elevation studies

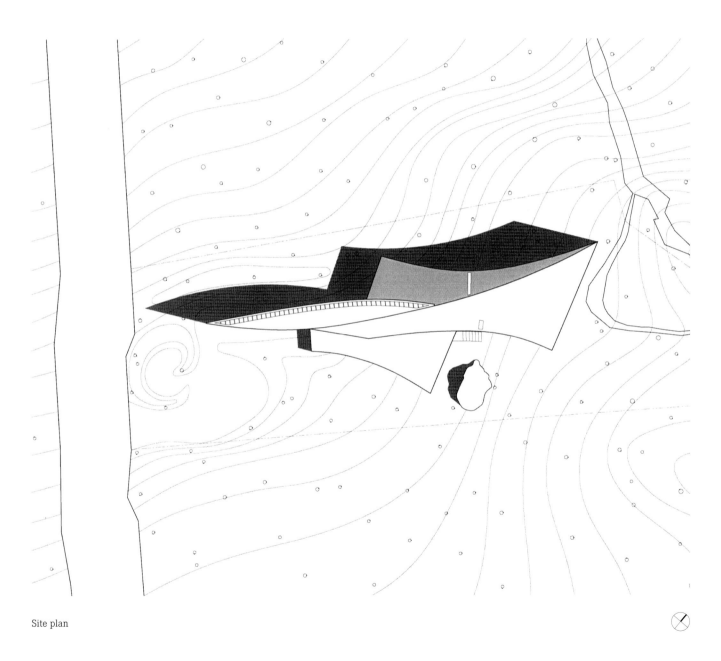

Site plan

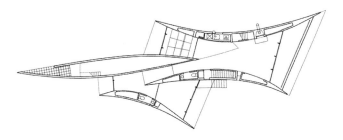

Ground floor

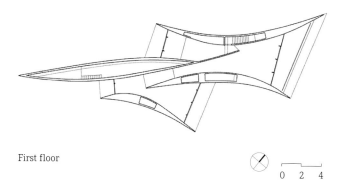

First floor

0   2   4

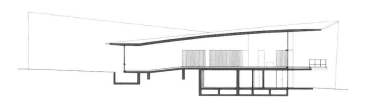

Longitudinal section

Transversal section

0   2   4

■ Satoshi Okada graduated in architecture at the University of Columbia, New York, in 1989. He studied there in 1997 under the tutorage of Kenneth Frampton. His international recognition came with his project of Mount Fuji, in 2000, which has been extensively studied. Today he works both as architect and teacher in the Environmental Design School, where he has founded the Institute of Design for Architecture and the Environment (IDEA). He is regularly invited as a teacher to different universities around the world.

Satoshi Okada
Architects

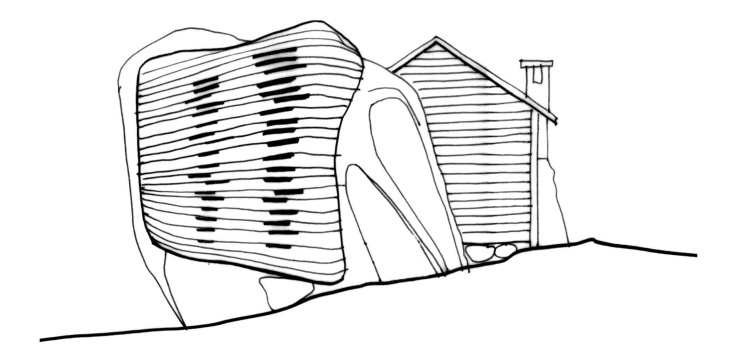

Budget: $ 100,000

■ This striking volume was built alongside a cabin that dates back to the last century, and is located in a forest reserve on the banks of a stream. It is an extension of the already existing building and is characterised by its use of wood, as both a structural system and as a material to clad both the interior and exterior. The new construction adapts to the weather conditions as well as the number of occupants thanks to an extending structure that offers double-cladding during the winter, or a roofed terrace in the summer. The analogies to the local fauna and to the textures of the surrounding forest have played a predominant role in the process of this design.

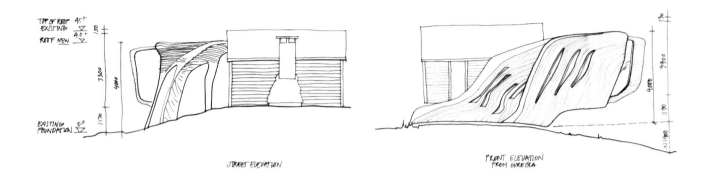

STREET ELEVATION

PRONT ELEVATION
FROM OURE GLA

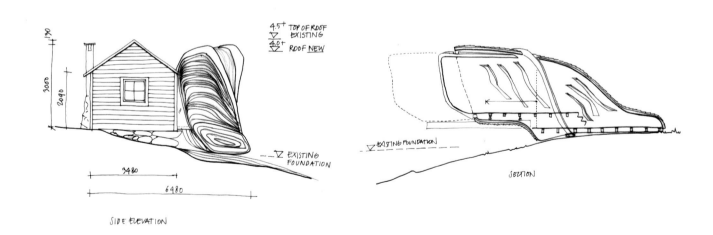

SIDE ELEVATION

SECTION

Preliminary sketches

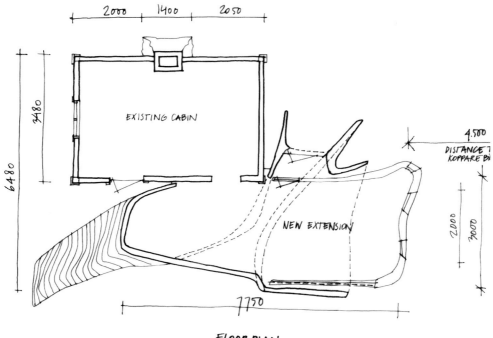

2000 | 1400 | 2050

3480

6480

EXISTING CABIN

NEW EXTENSION

4.500
DISTANCE
KOPPARE B

2000

3000

7750

FLOOR PLAN

Preliminary sketch

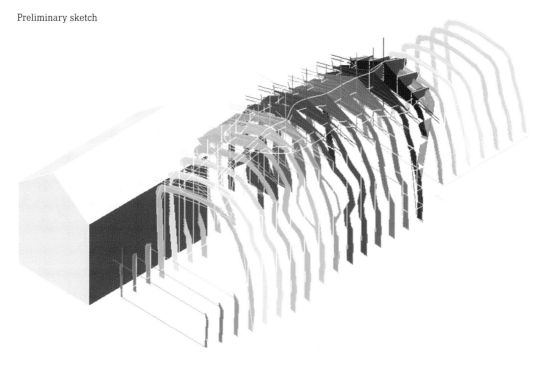

Structural diagram

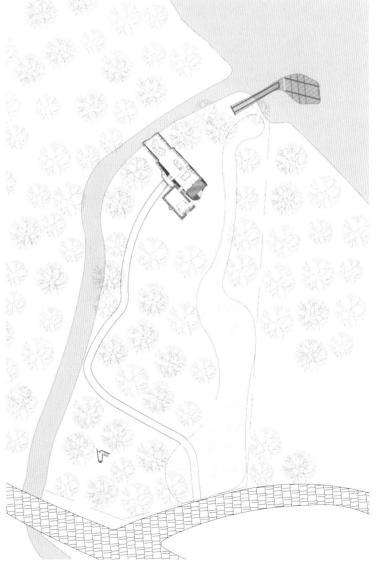

Site plan

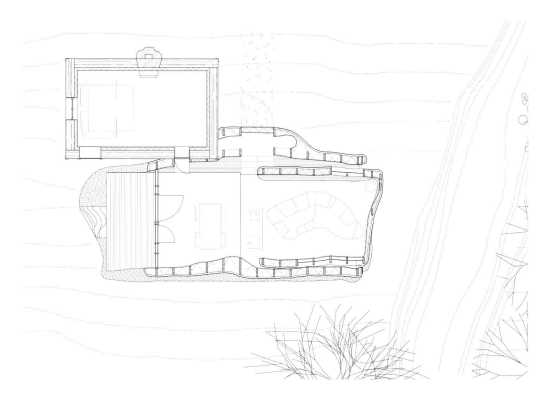

Plan (closed position)

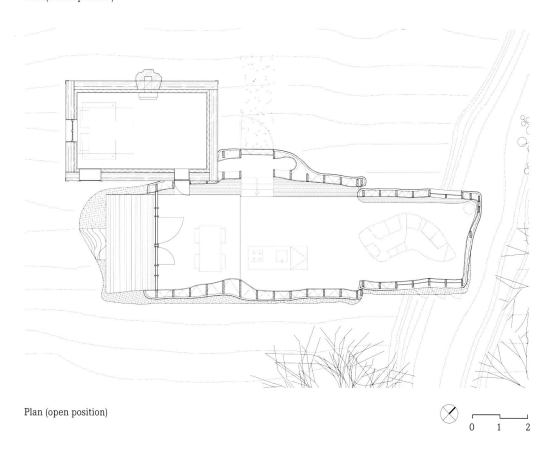

Plan (open position)

39

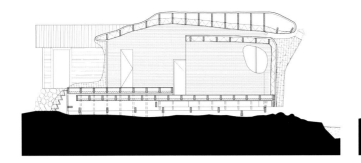

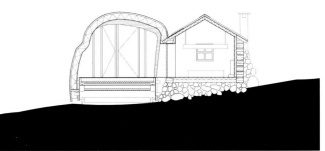

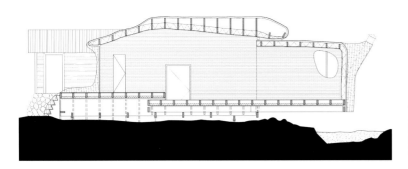

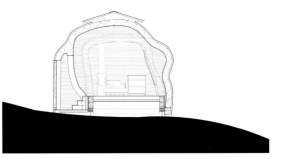

Sections

0 2 4

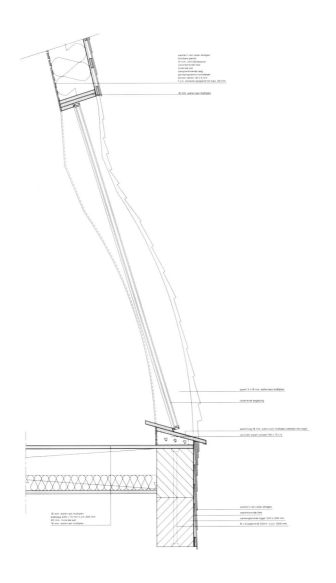

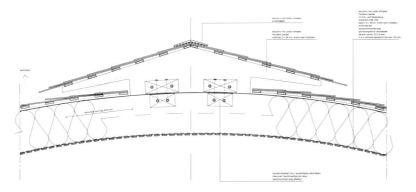

Construction details

■ Boris Zeisser and Maartje Lammers, after having collaborated with prestigious professionals in the field, such as the Office for Metropolitan Architecture (OMA), Mecanoo or Erick van Egeraat Architects, founded their own architecture and design company, 24H Architecture, in 2001. Right from the beginning they have carried out commissions of diverse scales, from houses to large urban plans. Their intention was to create a recognizable name, 24H, which encompasses different disciplines and can find solutions appropriate to each project.

24H Architecture

Bayer & Uhrig Architekten **House Göppner** Ramstein, Germany

Budget: $ 364,560

■ This house, situated in a cul-de sac, at first sight has the same appearance as the buildings around it; they are closed, white volumes with few openings, sloping roofs and include small adjacent buildings used as garages. However, behind this exterior image hides a different typology, a U-shaped plan that generates a large south-facing courtyard, towards which all the rooms in the house face. Another defining aspect is the parking, which instead of being an additional body, is a space taken from the main volume and also constitutes the access porch.

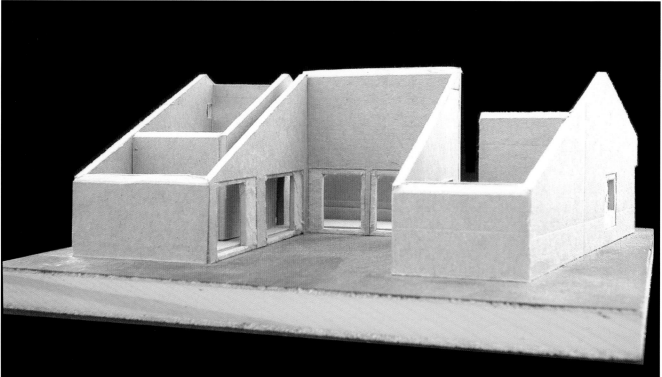

Models

Site plan

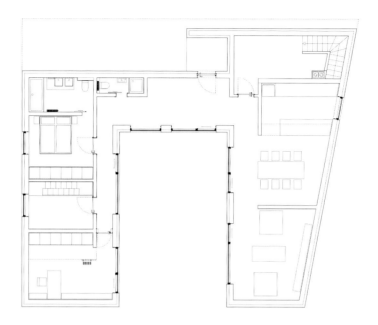

Ground floor

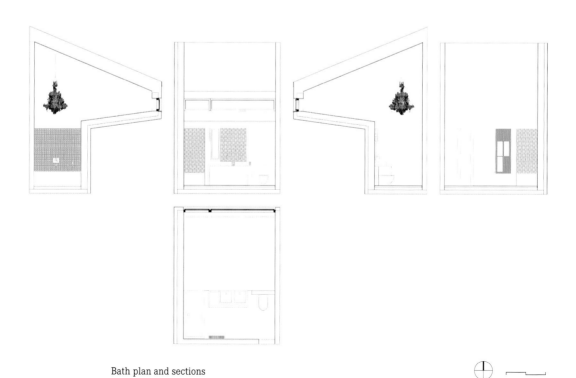

Bath plan and sections

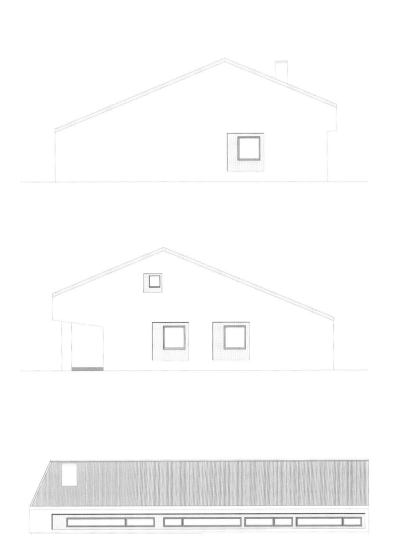

Elevations

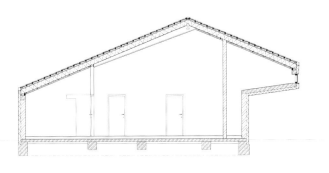

Transversal section

0   1   2

■ Dirk Bayer and Andrea Uhrig were born in Kaiserslautern, Germany, in 1968 and 1965, respectively. Both graduated in architecture at the technical university of this city in 1991. Both continued in academia, while collaborating with various architectural firms in Darmstadt, Munich and Vienna. In 2000 they founded their own architectural firm, Bayer & Uhrig Architekten, in their home city and where today they develop projects of highly diverse scales. They actively take part in teaching in various German and foreign universities.

**Bayer & Uhrig
Architekten**

Budget: $ 350,000

■ The design of this house had to follow the strict town-planning regulations that affect the centre of Paris, and at the same time respond to the wants of the clients: to preserve the front garden, along with the lime tree growing in it; create a transparency in order to be able to admire the small palace that occupies one end of the site; give emphasis to an enormous rock from the Parisian basin and, as well as plans common to a home, the clients wanted a home cinema and a guest pavilion. The project was structured on an enormous slab of concrete, raised 3.94 ft above street level, that spread across the entire surface of the site, and which could be shortened, drilled into or shaped according to the needs of the programme.

Models

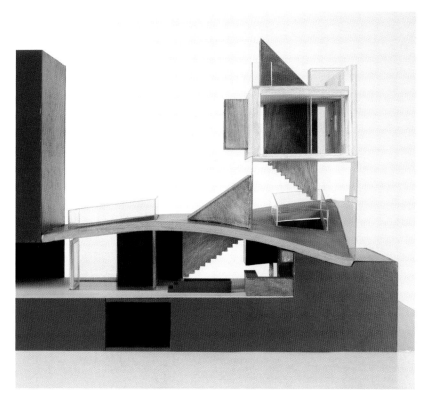

Models

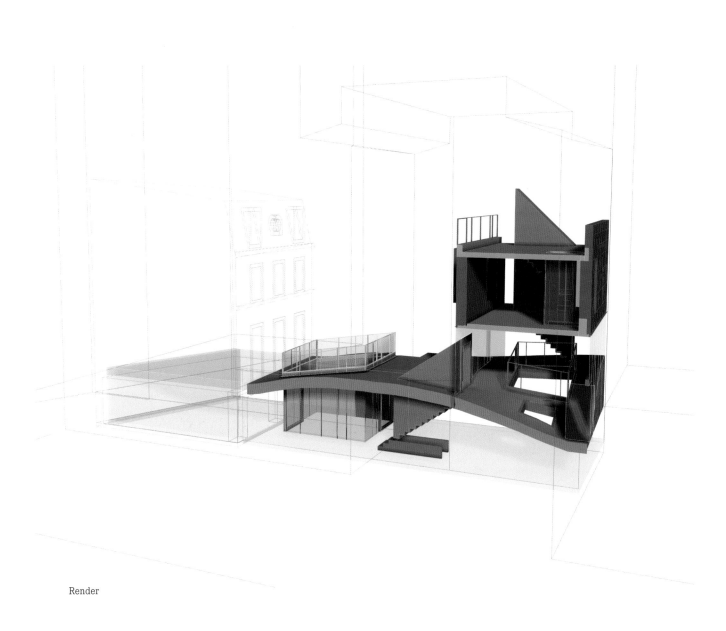

Render

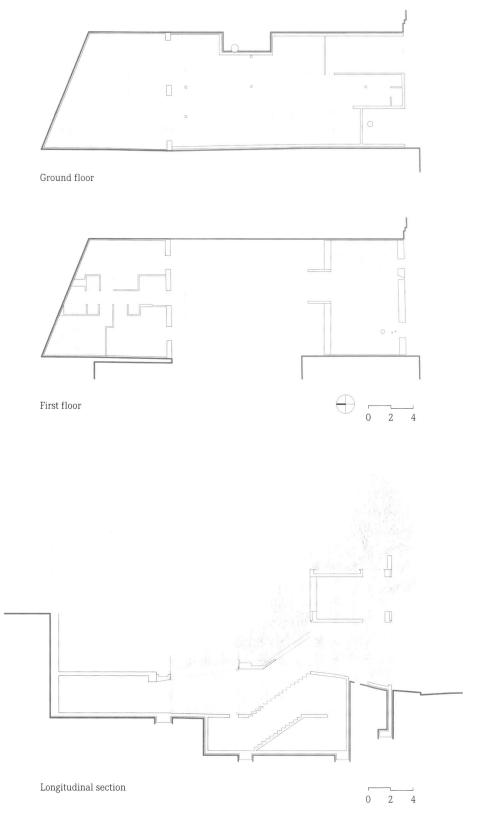

Ground floor

First floor

0   2   4

Longitudinal section

0   2   4

■ Christian Pottgiesser was born in Germany but, at a very early age, moved to Paris. He studied architecture in the Paris-Villemin School of Architecture and then his doctorate in Sorbonne. In this city, in 1991, he founded his own company were he worked on various projects, mainly residential, for Germany, Austria and France. He has been invited to take part in several international competitions and his work has been published equally over Europe, the United States and Japan.

Christian Pottgiesser

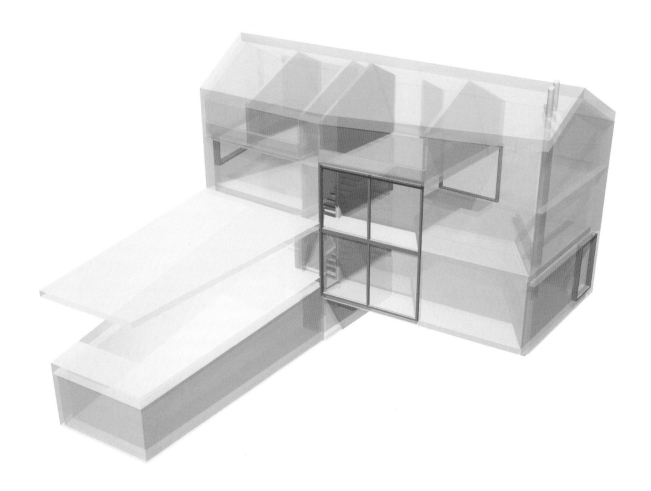

Budget: $ 400,000

■ Situated on the outskirts of Dornbirn, this house is surrounded by typical regional constructions, which are characterised by tiled gable roofs. Although it mimics the silhouette of the neighbouring buildings, this house stands out for its formal as much as constructive solution. From outside, the volume appears sculptural thanks to the absence of eaves on the façade, the exterior finish of stainless steel, on the façades as well as the roof, and the irregular composition of the large windows. Constructively, it comprises a concrete structure clad on the outside in perforated panels of stainless steel.

© Adolf Bereuter

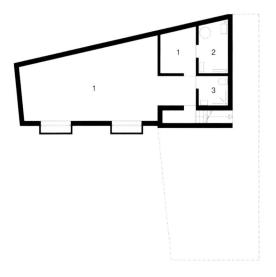

Basement

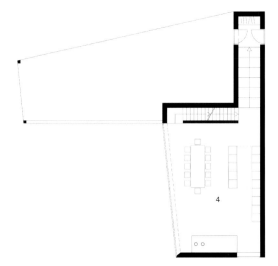

Ground floor

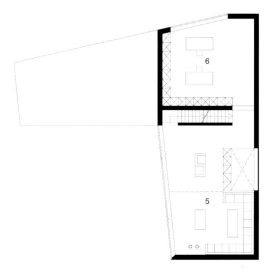

First floor

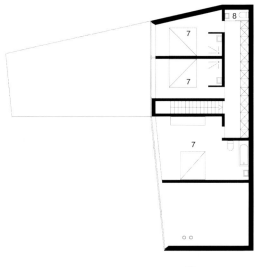

Second floor

0 1 2

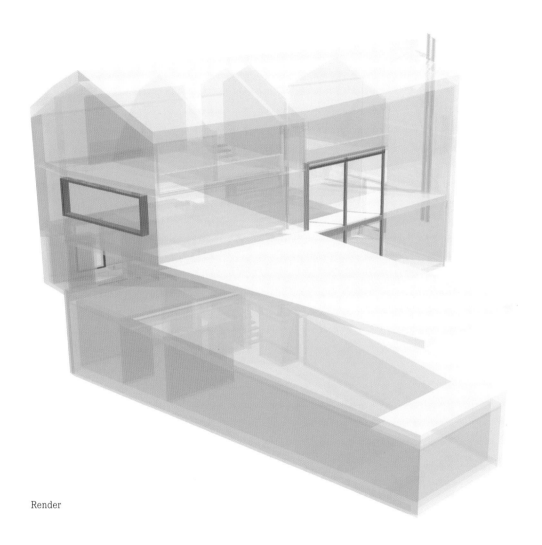

Render

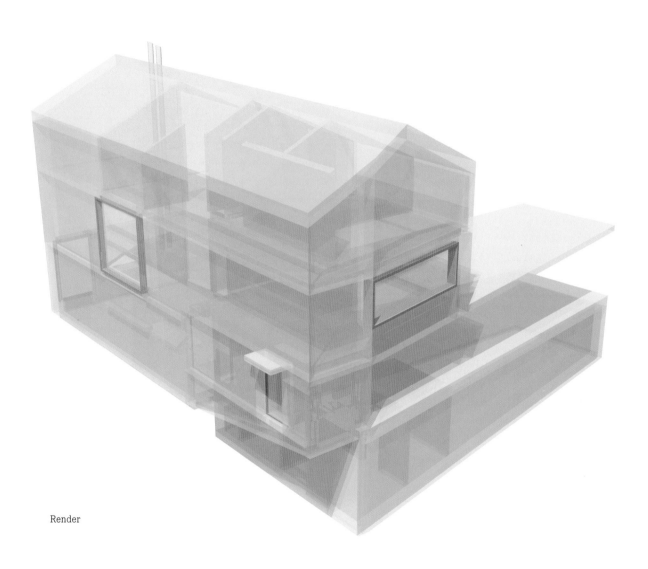

Render

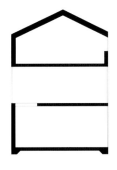

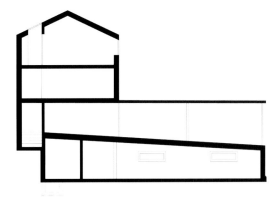

Transversal sections

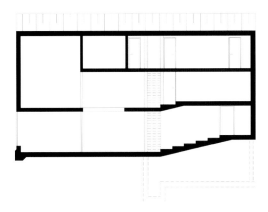

Longitudinal section

0 1 2

■ Oskar Leo Kaufmann was born in Bregenz, Austria, in 1969. In 1995 he graduated in architecture in the Technical University of Vienna. After working alongside Johannes Kaufmann, he created his own architectural firm in 2001. Today he develops projects with specialist, Albert Rüf. His work, which is noteworthy for employing new technologies to increase the flexibility and versatility of each building, is focused primarily on the design of single-family homes and medium scale projects.

Oskar Leo Kaufmann

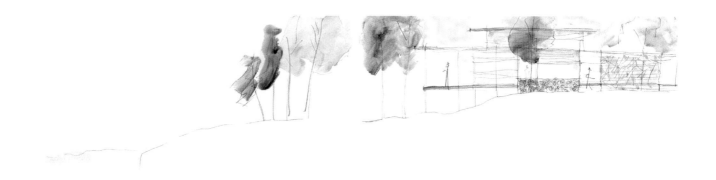

Budget: $ 350,000

■ The clients of this recreational house, both partners and art collectors, wanted a rural refuge, immersed in nature, with a space especially designed for exhibiting their varied repertoire of sculptures. The plot is situated in a wide valley, populated by a dense pine forest and a few metres from the river. Town planning regulations and the fragile surroundings were factors that determined the design of this project. Wood was the predominant material used here in the structure, the interior finishes, the carpentry and the furniture, all with the aim of maximising the integration with the landscape.

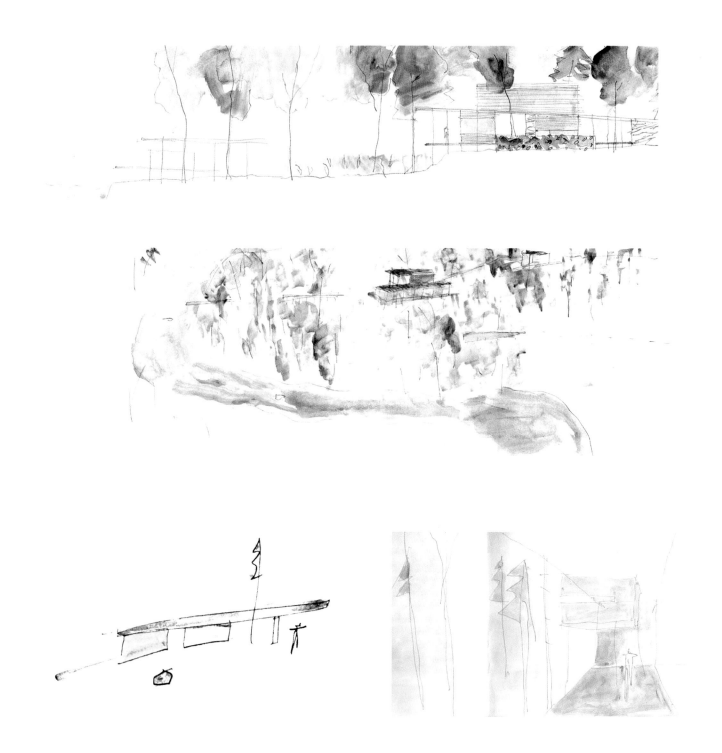

Preliminary sketches

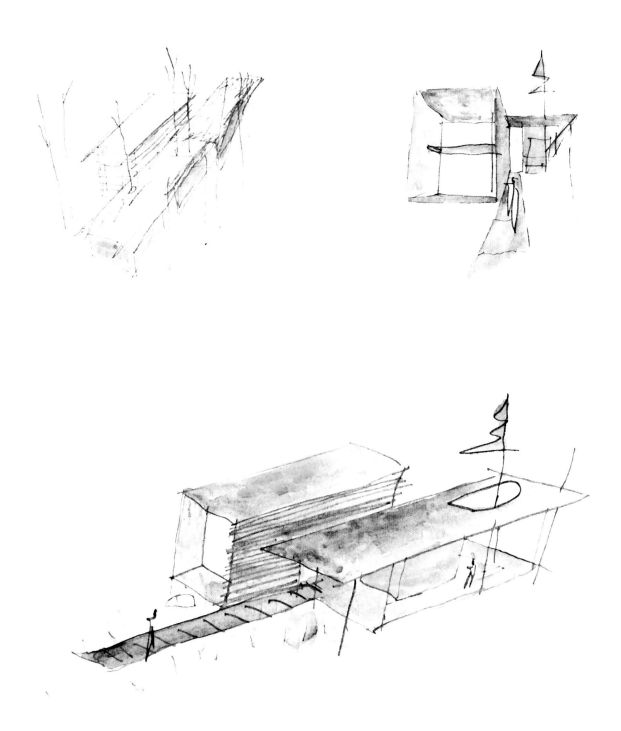

Preliminary sketches

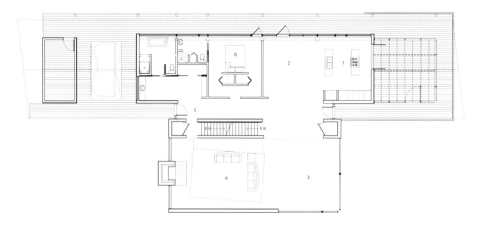

Ground floor

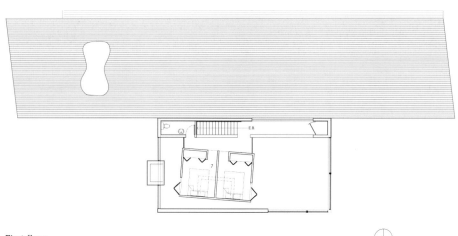

First floor

0   2   4

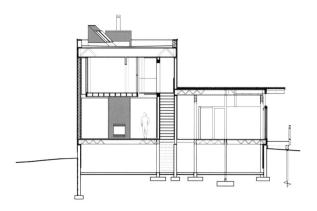

Transversal section

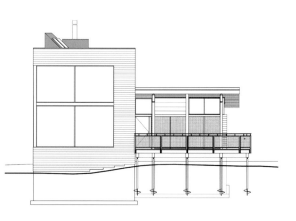

Elevation

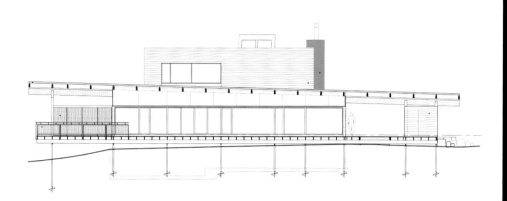

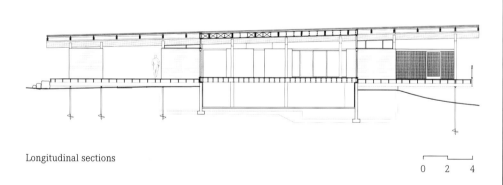

Longitudinal sections

0   2   4

■ Pierre Thibault has been giving classes in architecture at the University of Laval, in Québec, since 1982. His work is characterised by his environmentally friendly solutions, which meet the clients' needs, and by all the types of environments he has dealt with. His early work, in landscaping and institutional design, received awards in Canada, United States and Europe. Today he works with a large team of collaborators, professionals and specialists, with whom he tackles varying scales and typologies of projects.

Pierre Thibault

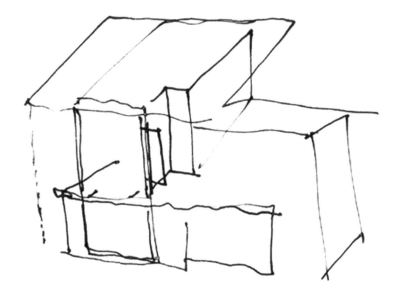

Budget: $ 550,000

■ The design of this house had to resolve a series of difficulties that characterise its long history. To start with, it was a house from the seventies, onto which an extension had been started, which then had to be suspended for personal reasons of the client. Seven years later, on returning to this task, bylaws and other obstacles meant they were unable to finish the project. The great challenge for Pugh & Scarpa was to devise a modern project that resolved the needs of the family, was in accordance with the regulations, and furthermore used the existing foundations.

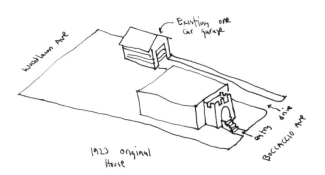

THRU - LOT = street both sides
entry on Boccaccio

Woodlawn Ave

Existing one
car garage

Boccaccio Ave

entry drive

1923 original
House

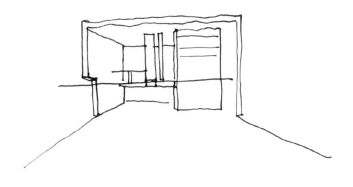

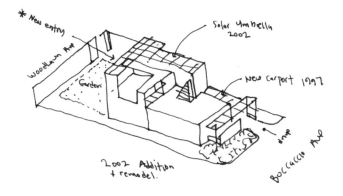

* New entry

Woodlawn Ave

Garden

Solar Umbrella
2002

New carport 1997

ramp

Boccaccio Ave

2002 Addition
+ remodel.

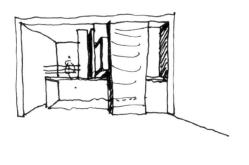

Preliminary sketches

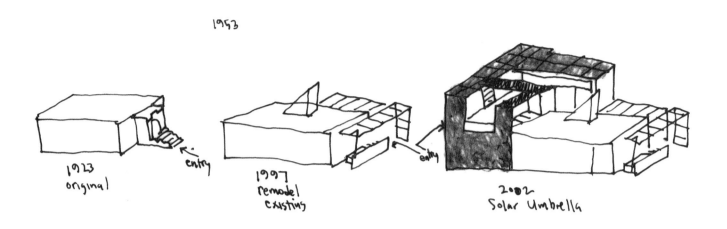

1953

1923
original

entry

1997
remodel
existing

entry

2002
Solar Umbrella

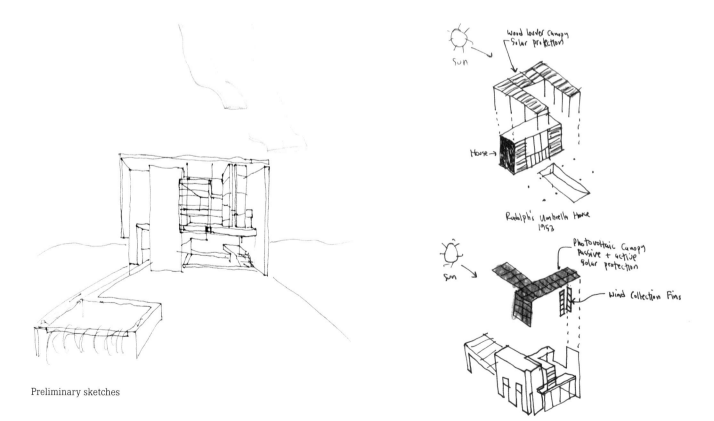

Preliminary sketches

Sun

Wood louver canopy
(solar protection)

House →

Rudolph's Umbrella House
1953

Sun

Photovoltaic Canopy
Passive + active
solar protection

Wind Collection Fins

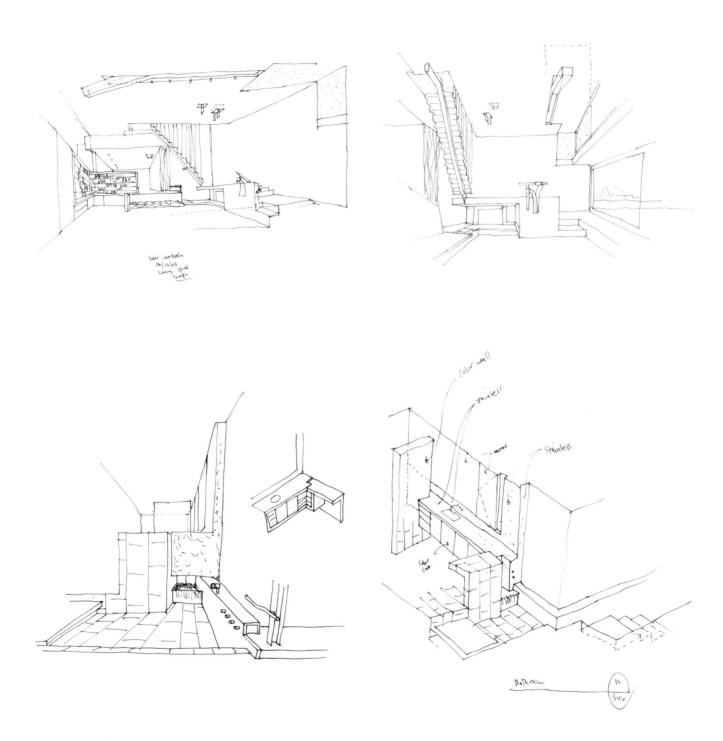

Interior perspectives

Elevation study

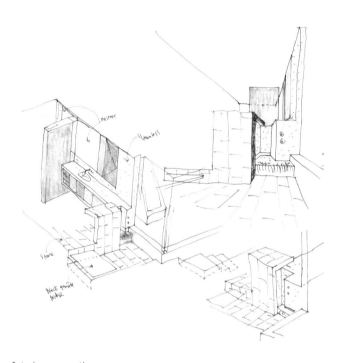
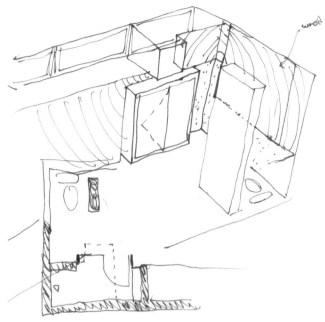

Interior perspectives

Models

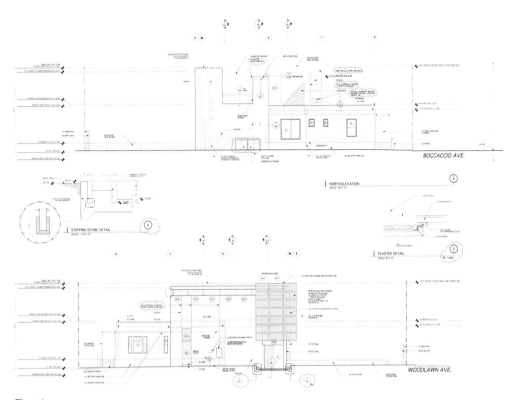

Elevations

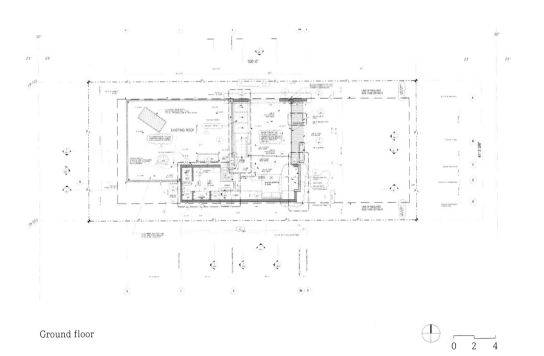

Ground floor

Roof plan

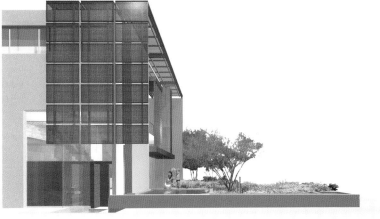

Perspectives

Section

0 2 4

Pugh & Scarpa's studio was set up in 1991 in Santa Mónica, California. Its infrastructure and philosophy, which attempts to rethink all design processes of a project, allows them to take on a wide range of commissions in architecture, engineering, interior design and town-planning. Today, 22 professionals with varying disciplines work for the firm finding solutions to public projects. As well as their office in Santa Monica, they have a subsidiary in Charlotte, North Carolina.

Pugh & Scarpa

OOS **Schudel House** Feldis, Switzerland

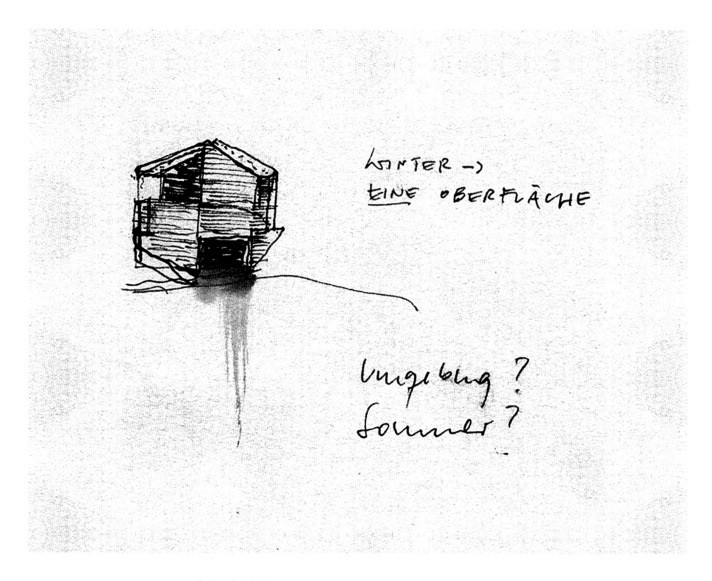

Budget: $ 550,000

■ The location of this house is characterised by the pronounced slope of the plot, the extraordinary surrounding mountains and the spectacular views of the valley. The new construction built with local wood makes it a distinctive volume, formally expressive and firmly anchored to the rocky terrain of the plot. The monolithic shape of this recreational home assumes different appearances —narrow and light, large and heavy— depending on which angle you see it from. The open positioning of the large Venetian windows completely changes the house's exterior aspect.

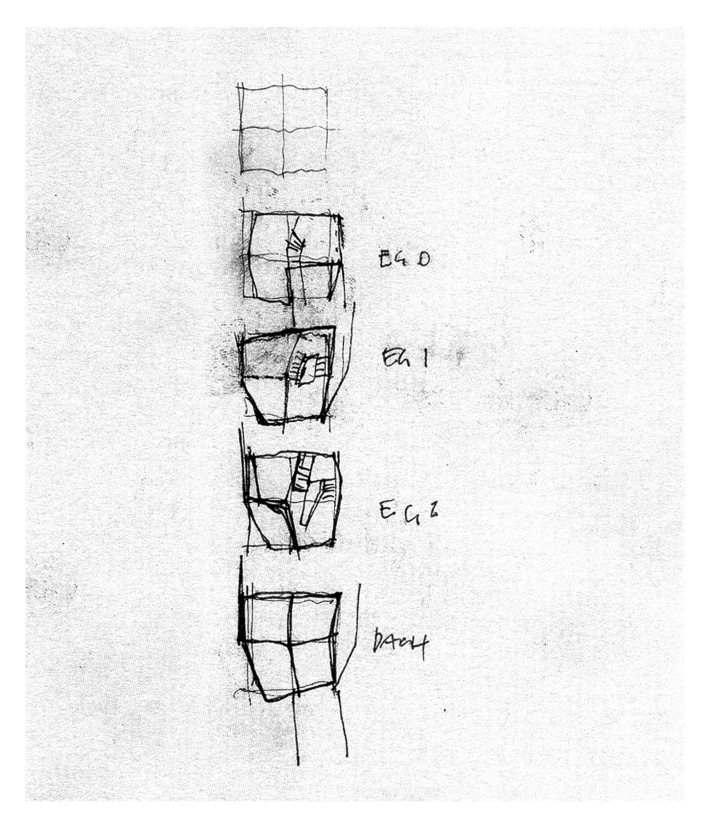

EG 0

EG 1

EG 2

DACH

Preliminary sketches

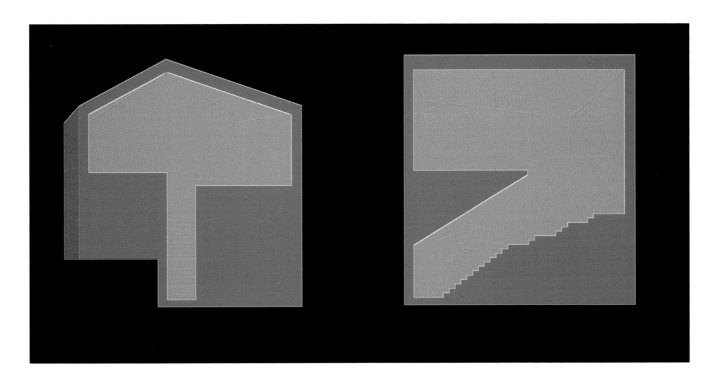

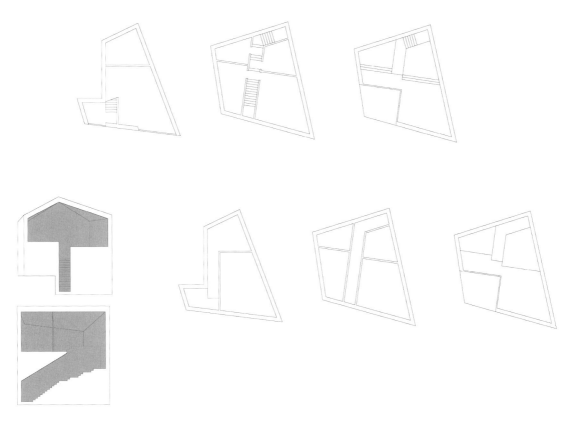

Distribution diagrams

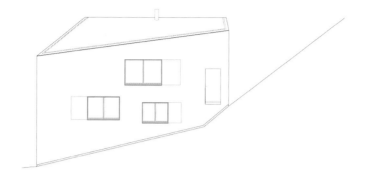

East elevation

West elevation

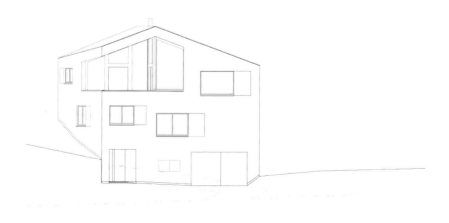

South elevation

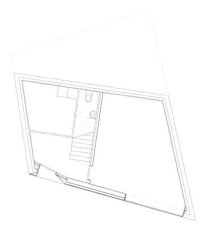

Ground floor

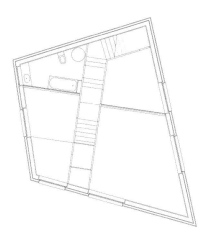

First floor

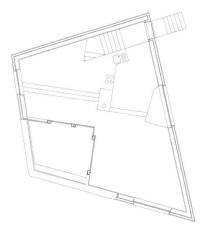

Second floor

0   2   4

■ OOS is an architectural firm established in Zürich, Switzerland by Andreas Derrer, Lukas Bosshard, Christoph Kellenberger and Severin Boser in 2000. It specialises in urban development and renders services from consultancy and investment appraisals, to design, development, planning and construction. Their aim is to produce architecture of high quality, while at the same time to deliver economically consistent results. Their work has earned them various international architecture and design awards.

OOS

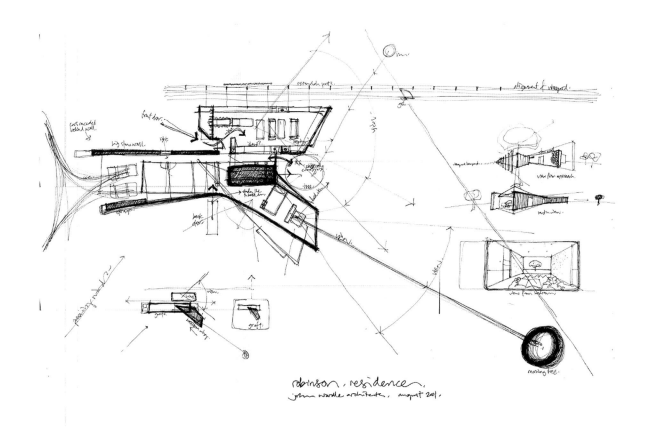

■ This house is situated in a large area of vineyards and responds to the clients' desire to move their permanent home from the city to the country. The building's position within the site and its volumes was defined as much by the ordered rows of grapevines as the desire to have views over the countryside. The structure is made up of robust wooden columns that support a light metal framework, which forms the upper part of the building. The properties of each material combine to create a project whose spaces are highly expressive, and which interacts with the surroundings. The house won the Harold Desbrowe-Annear award, given by the Royal Australian Institute of Architects, for the best residential project of 2004.

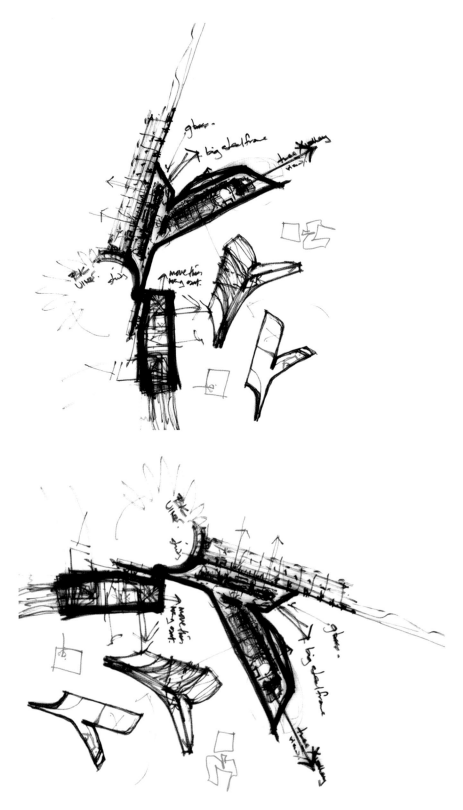

Preliminary sketches

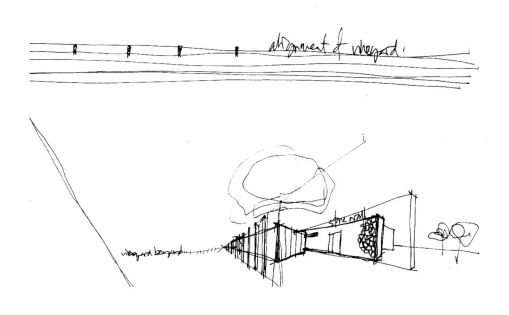

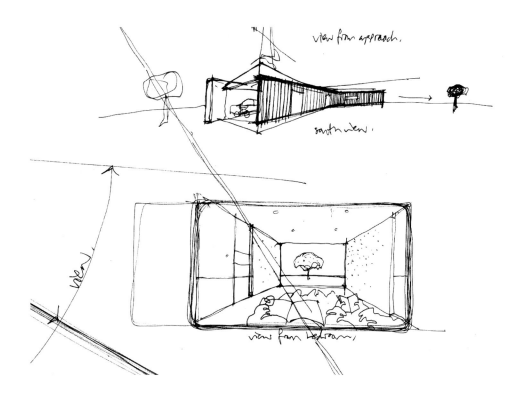

Perspective studies

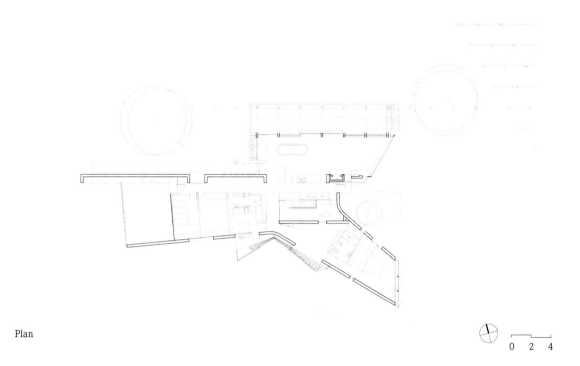

Plan

0 2 4

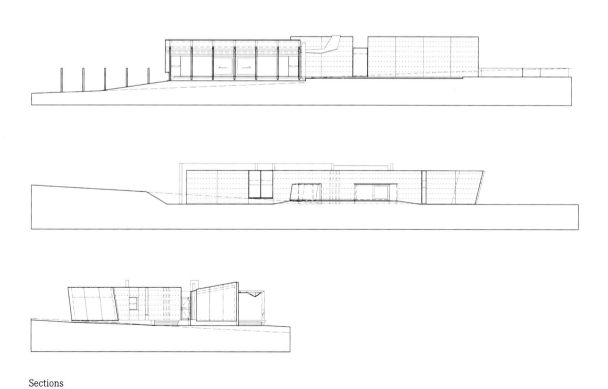

Sections

0 2 4

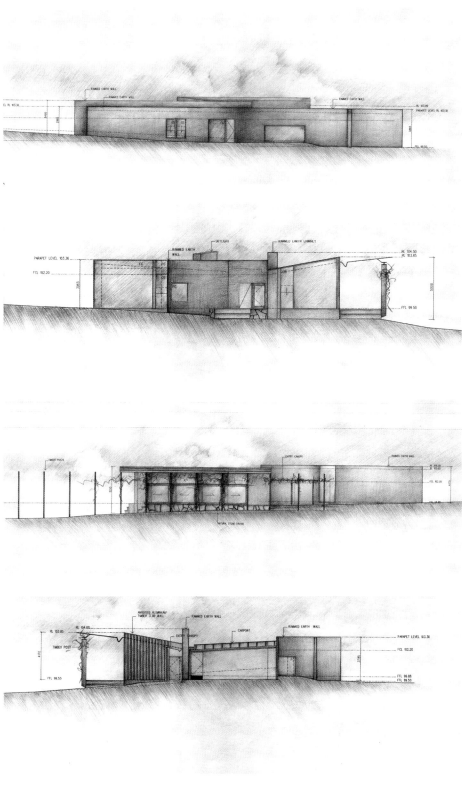

■ John Wardle Architects, founded in 1986 by Wardle himself, today comprises 21 professionals who collaborate in diverse disciplines. This firm stands out for the hugely varying scales of its projects carried out all over Australia. Their work includes single family houses, apartment blocks, university buildings, offices and commercial centres. The particular characteristics of each client are used to enrich and personalize each project.

Elevations

John Wardle Architects

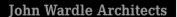

Waro Kishi **House in Higashi-Otsu** Higashi-Otsu, Shiga, Japan

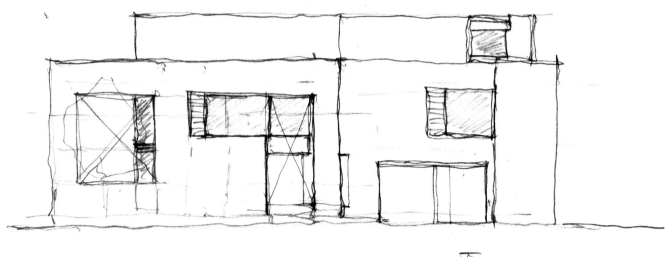

FACADE

01/12/17

■ This house answers a request to house two generations of the same family. The segregation within the house is resolved via a circulation that permanently links the exterior, using terraces or large windows. The house has three stories: one onto the street containing the parking and the amenities; the first floor, which primarily caters for the younger members of the family, and the second floor, with the living area and parents' rooms. The orthogonal geometrics are interrupted because of the diagonal plan, which shows the borders of the plot and encloses the exterior areas.

© Hiroyuki Hirai

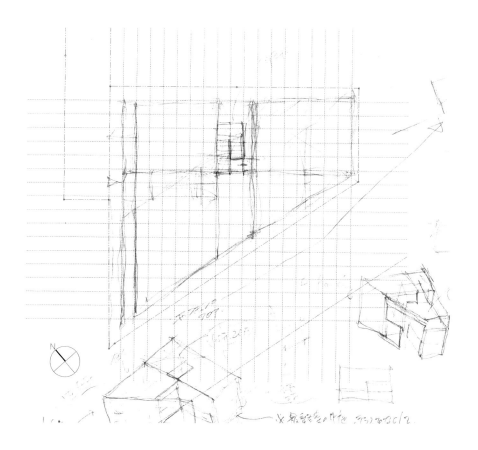

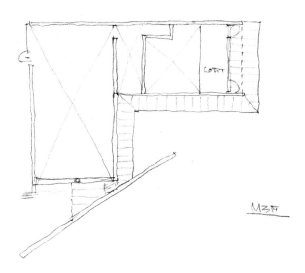

Preliminary sketches

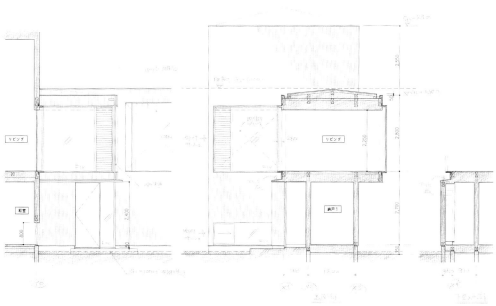

Transversal section

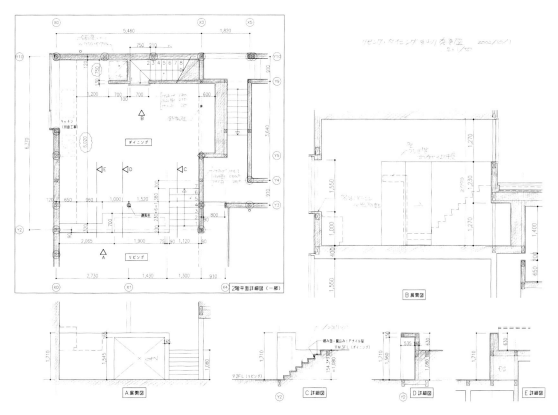

Detailed studies

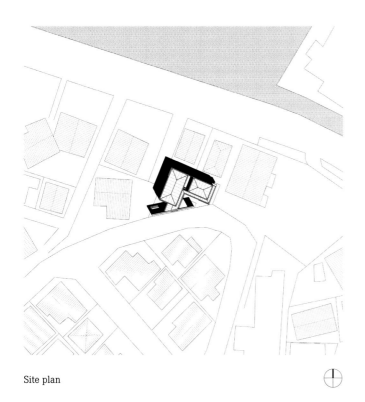

Site plan

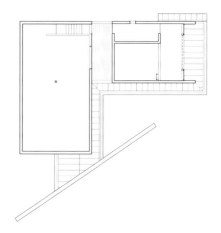

Ground floor

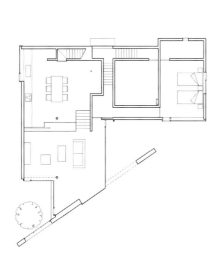

First floor

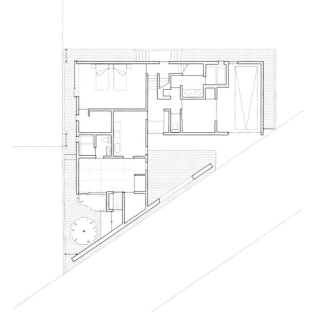

Second floor

0 2 4

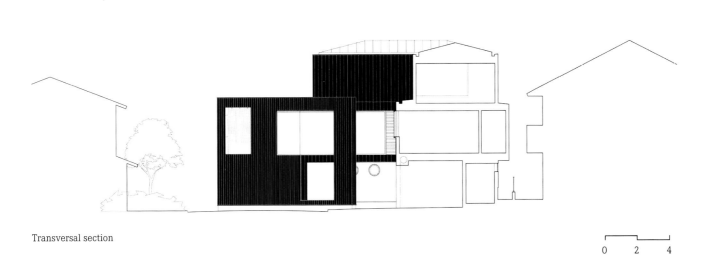

Transversal section

0   2   4

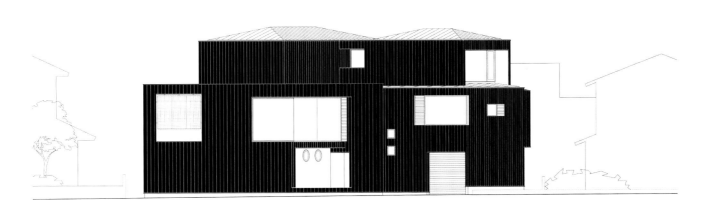

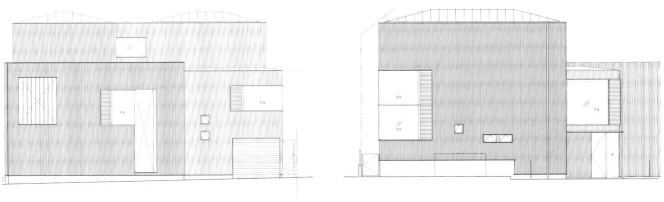

Elevations

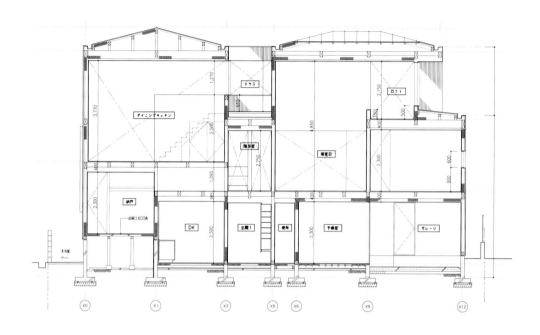

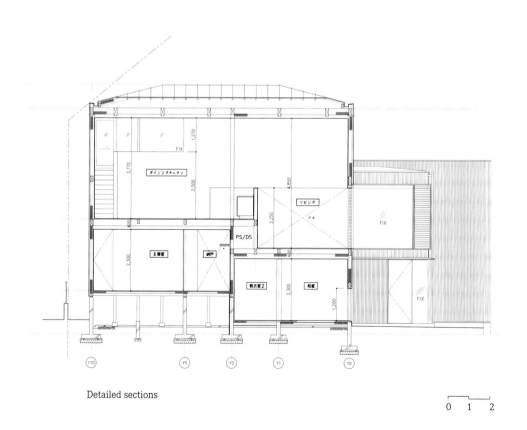

Detailed sections

0   1   2

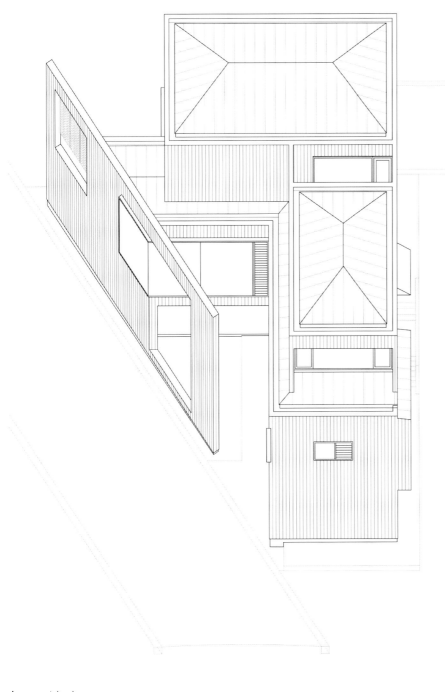

Axonometric view

■ Waro Kishi was born in Yokohama, Japan, in 1950 and first graduated from the faculty of electronics, in 1973 and later in architecture, in 1975, in the University of Kyoto. He has maintained links with this university, firstly by finishing his studies with a post grad in architecture, and then as a teacher. He has also given classes in the University of Berkeley, California, and in the Massachusetts Institute of Technology (MIT), in Cambridge. In 1981 he founded his own architectural firm with which he has developed a wide variety of residential and commercial projects.

Waro Kishi

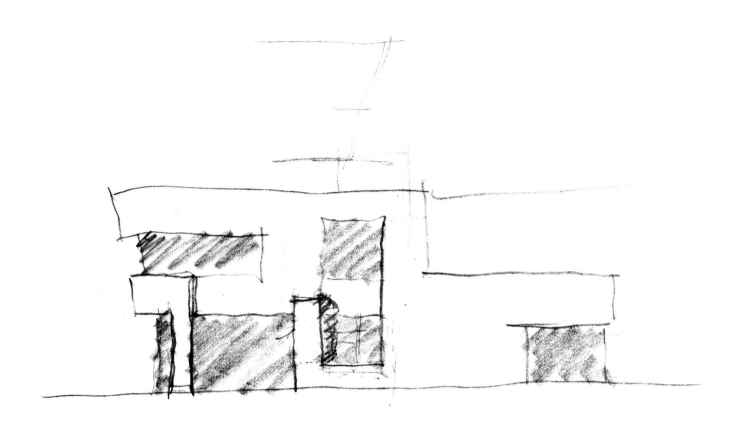

■ This house is situated on the edge of a cliff overlooking the Pacific Ocean, and began with an existing façade, which dates back to the 1950s. The restoration project, conceived originally by the late Frank Israel, was developed by his colleagues Barbara Callas and Steven Shortridge. A single-story volume can be seen from the access façade, but behind which the rest of the house slides down the plot to reveal two stories at the back end of the site. The inclination of the house's parameter walls emphasises the architect's intention to open the interior to the panoramic sea views.

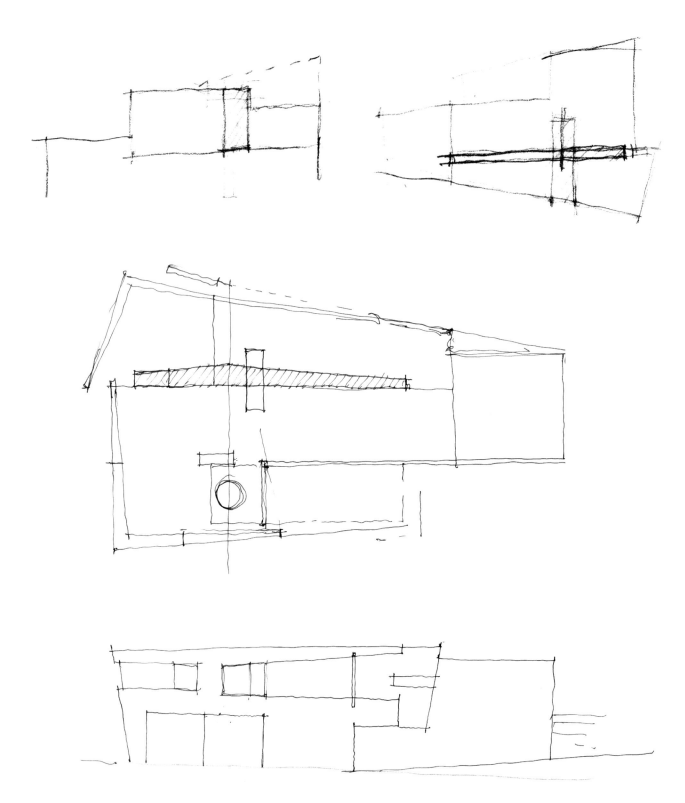

Preliminary sketches

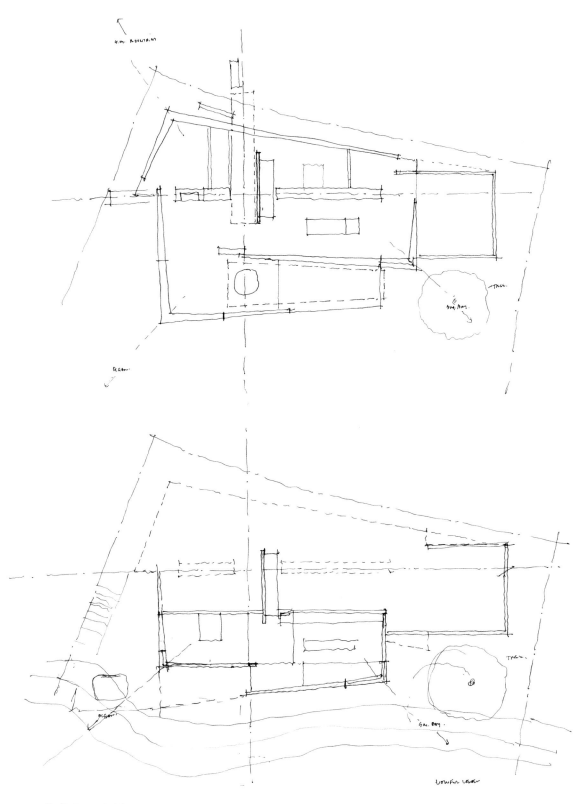

Preliminary sketches

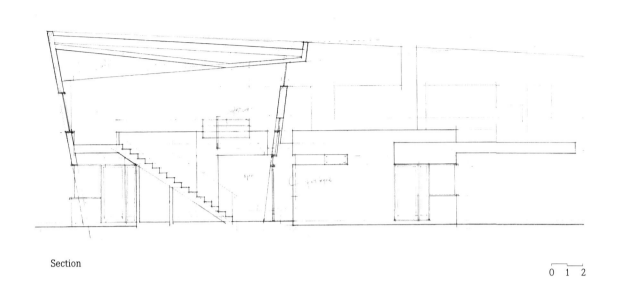

Section

0 1 2

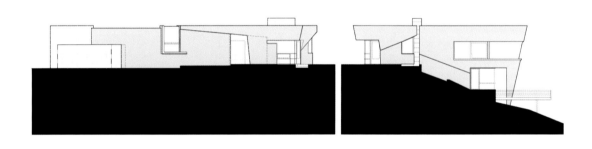

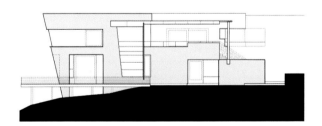

Elevations

Site plan

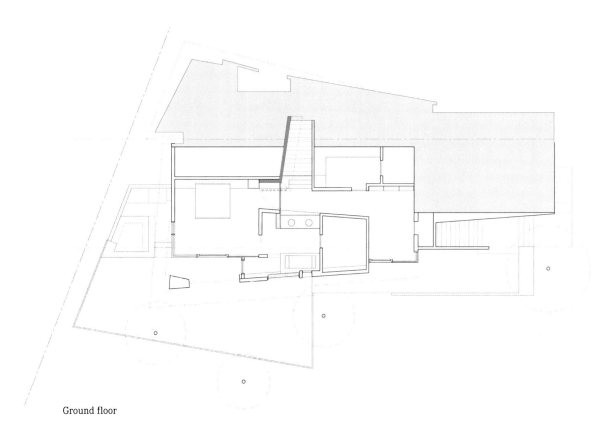

Ground floor

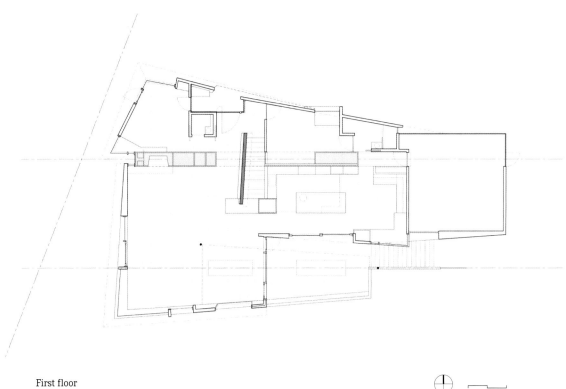

First floor

0 2 4

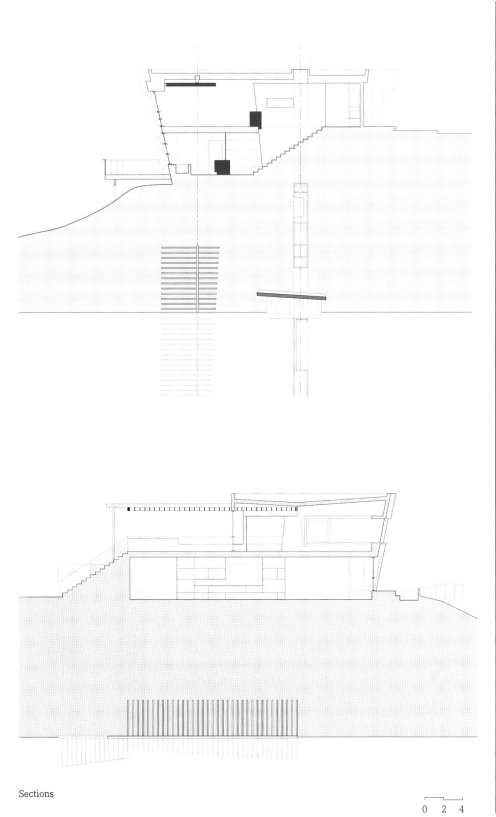

Sections

0   2   4

The firm Callas Shortridge Architects has been in existence since 1996. Its founders, Steven Shortridge and Barbara Callas were associates in the firm Israel Design Associates, in Beverly Hills. Before setting up their own studio, both had collaborated as architects, developing a wide variety of projects of different scales. Barbara is responsible for the development of projects that require in depth technical knowledge. Steven is responsible for managing the design and construction process for the firm's different projects. Both have received many prestigious design awards for their work.

Callas Shortridge
Architects

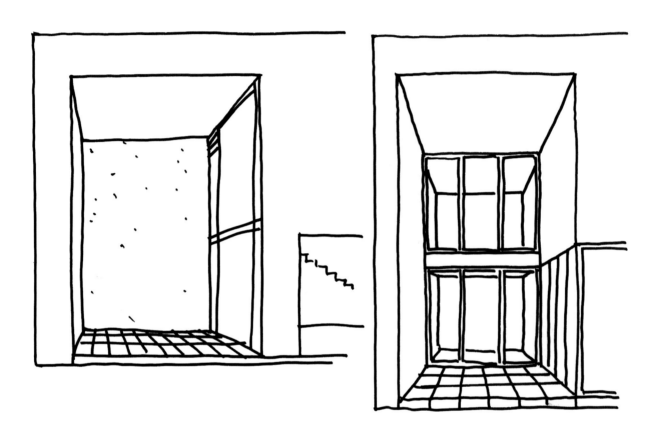

Budget: $ 380,000

■ This house was extended to include a volume for the owners' son, which has an independent access. There are two bedrooms sitting one on top of the other each with their own bathroom, and a kitchen situated by the entrance, with access to the garage, and separated from the dining room by a sliding door. The dining room, measuring twice the height of the other rooms, receives natural light that enters the large 33.6 ft wide by 8.2 ft high window. A set of stairs leads to the upper floor and to a panoramic balcony, which the upstairs bedroom has access to.

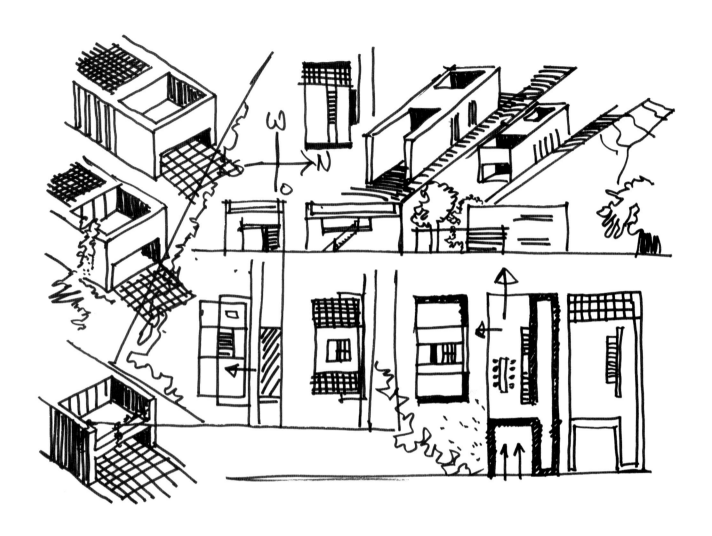

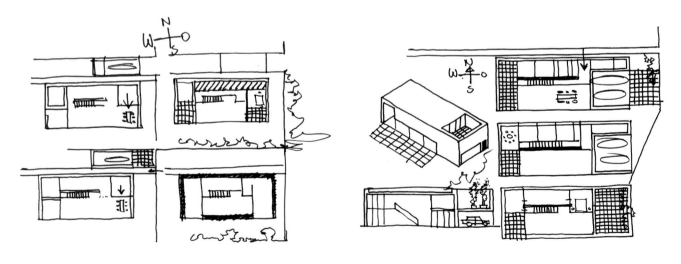

Preliminary sketches

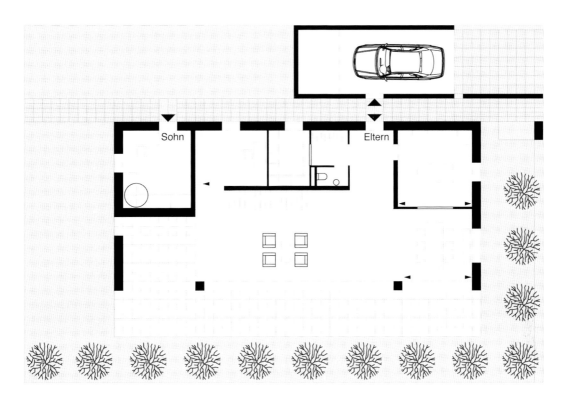

Ground floor

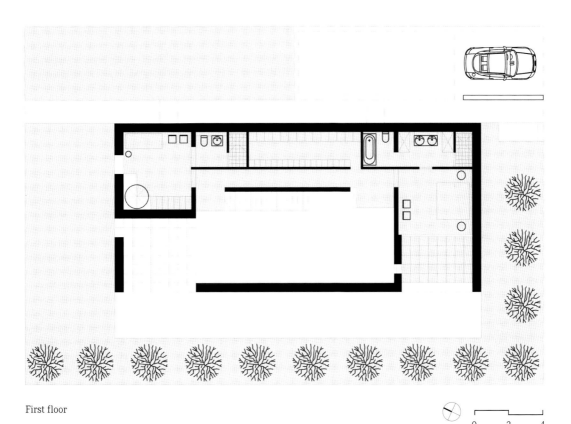

First floor

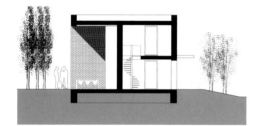

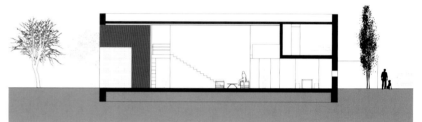

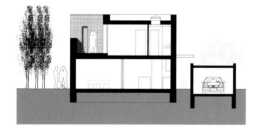

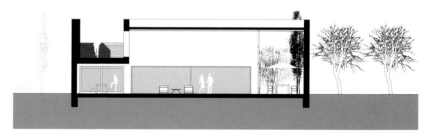

Sections

0   2   4

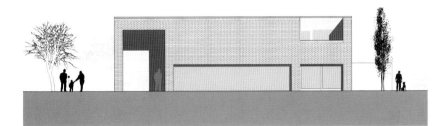

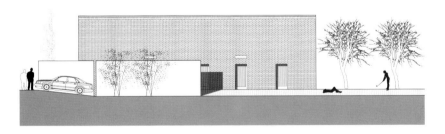

Elevations

■ Founded in Düsseldorf in 1996, the firm DDJ comprises the renowned architect Wolfgang Döring, Michael Dahmen and Elmar Joeressen, whose training and professional activity are closely linked to the former's. Wolfgang Döring's professional career is dominated by numerous exhibitions and publications he has taken part in. He is internationally recognised and is responsible for the Modena Cultural Centre and various sports centres in Saudi Arabia, as well as the drainage of the old quarter of Istanbul and Moscow's Constructivism Museum. He has been honorary professor and guest at the University of Tokyo and Buenos Aires.

**Döring
Dahmen Joeressen**

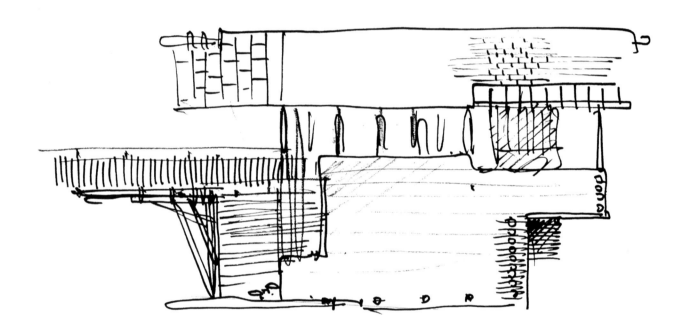

■ The project for this house, situated on the banks of Lake Muskoka, to the north of Toronto, attempted to find the balance between construction and landscape, and in turn, the traditional and the modern. Innovative design concepts and traditional construction techniques join forces to create a house, which draws on different aspects of the place: the granite that emerged after the last ice-age, pioneers' cabins, Victorian refuges, and wooden ships built by local craftsmen. Apart from its modest layout, the house accommodates two interior berths, one exterior roofed berth and a storage room for nautical material. It also has several terraces and a moss garden.

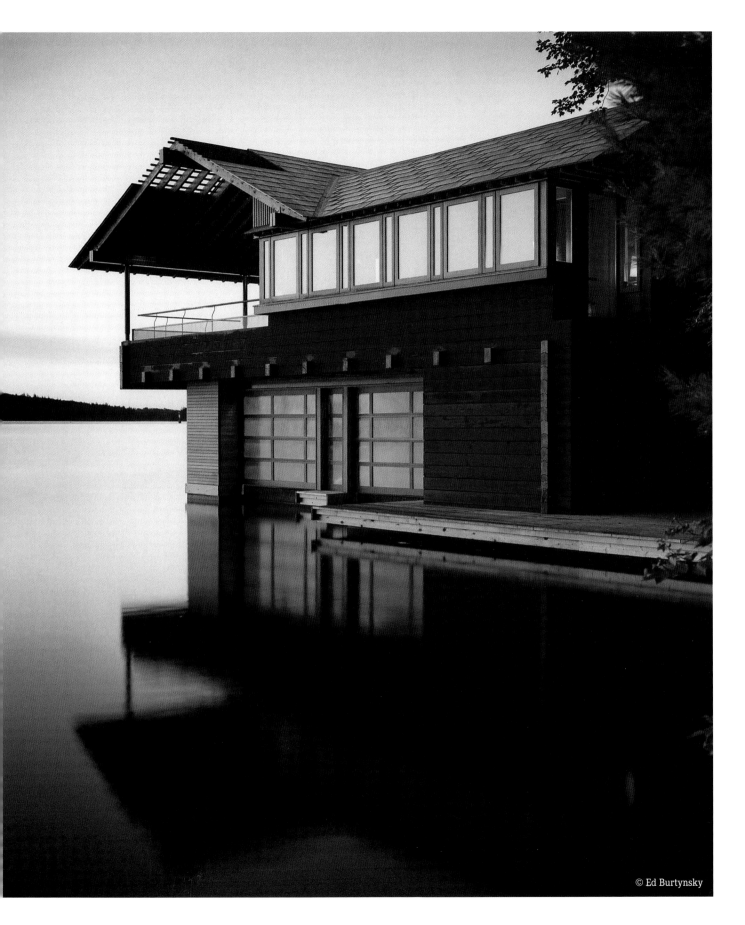

Preliminary sketches

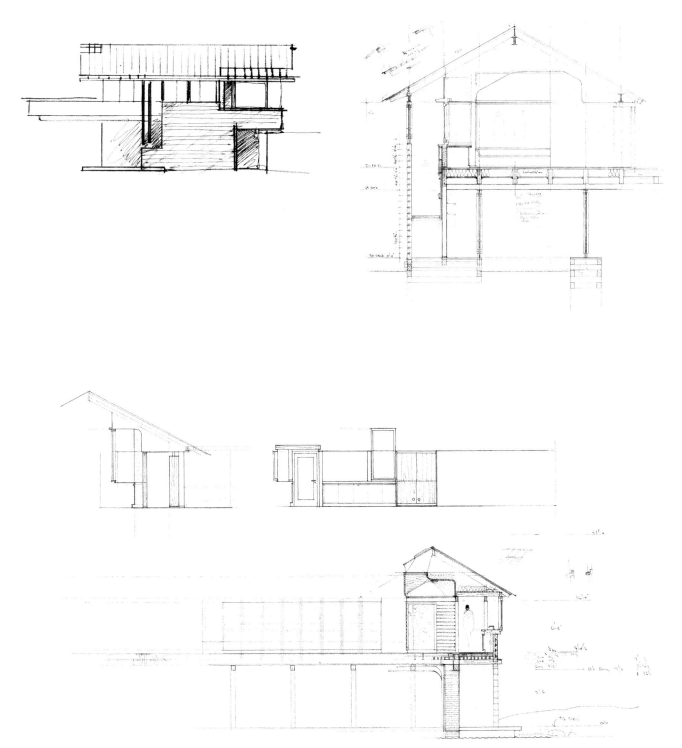

Section studies

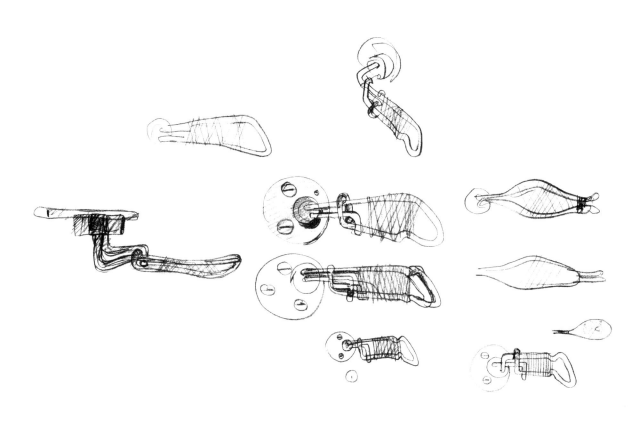

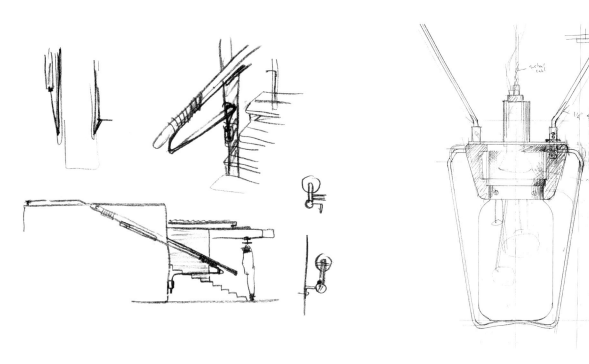

Detailed sketches

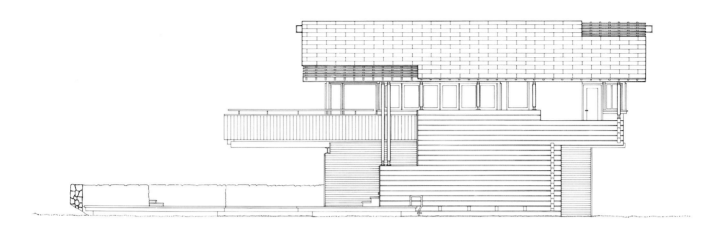

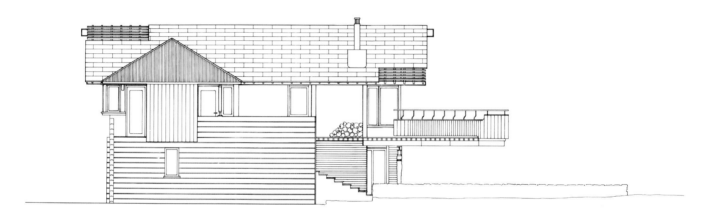

Elevations

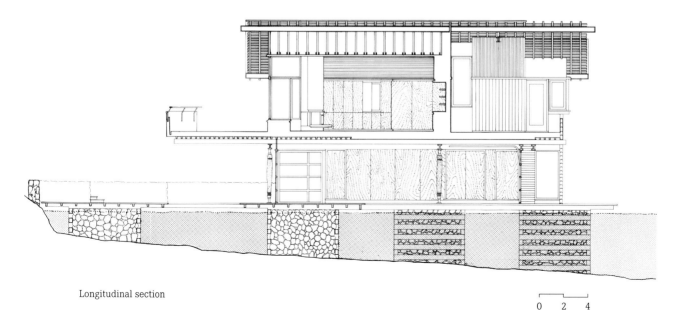

Longitudinal section

0 2 4

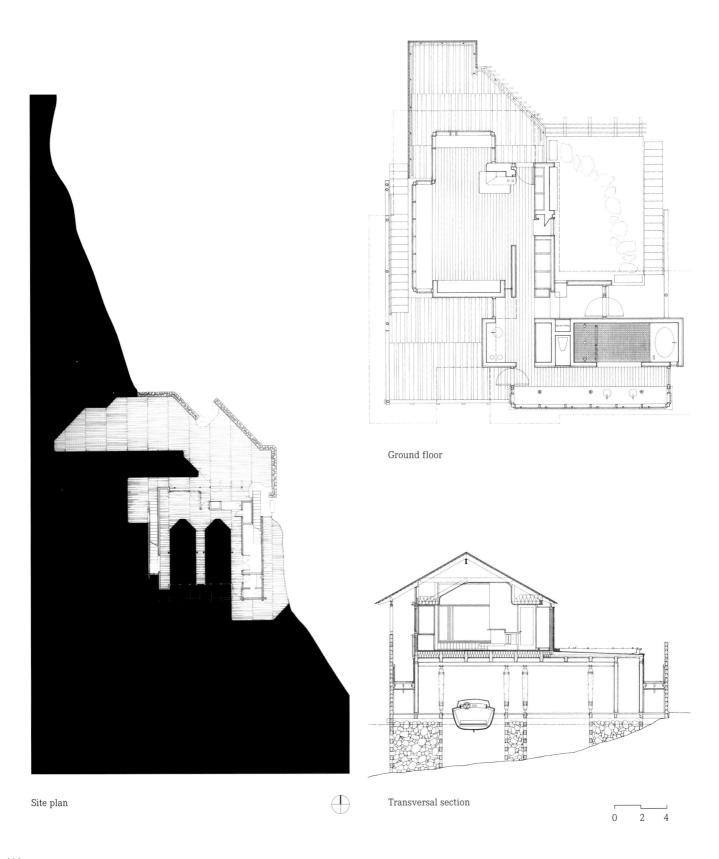

Ground floor

Site plan

Transversal section

0 2 4

Elevation

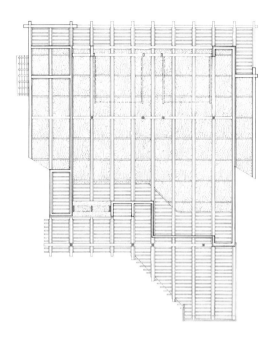

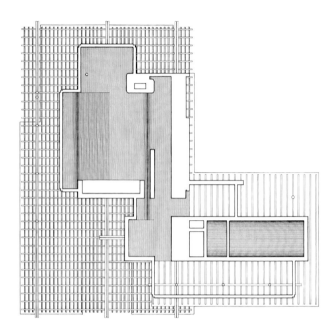

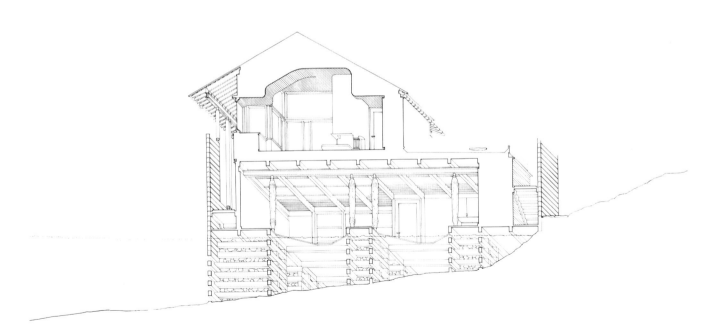

Structure studies

■ Briditte Shim, from Kingston (Jamaica), and Howard Sutcliffe, from Yorkshire (England), were born in 1958 and graduated in Environmental Studies and Architecture at Waterloo University. After collaborating with various prestigious architects in Canada they founded their own firm, Shim Sutcliffe Architects, with the aim of giving free rein to their passion for architecture, the environment and furniture. Their work is characterised by their constant search for relations between the object and the land, the building and the landscape, man and nature.

Shim Sutcliffe
Architects

Sketch by Howard Sutcliffe

Printed from a Photomechanical Tranfer
Original drawing in the collection of the
Centre Canadien d'Architecture/Canadian
Center for Architecture, Montreal
© Shim Sutcliffe Architects

Felipe Assadi **Schmitz House** Santiago, Chile

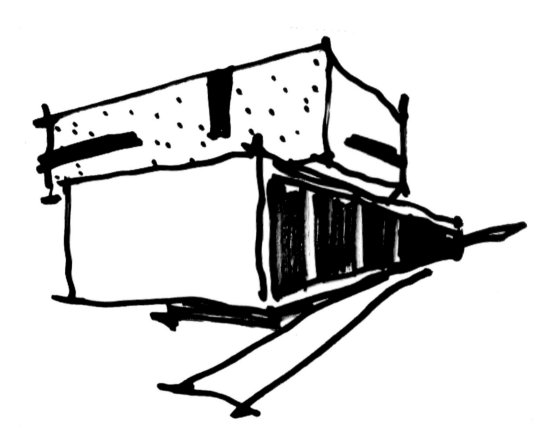

Budget: $ 350,000

■ A plantation of low fruit trees and the panoramic backdrop of the Andes determined the design of this house. The arrangement and rhythm of the trees suggested a certain direction and structural module, while their foliage, a metre above the ground, gave a new ground level to be able to admire the distant views. A reinforced concrete box along the east-west axis constitutes the foundations of the house and houses the swimming pool and basement. On top of this, at the height of the treetops is the first glazed volume containing the communal areas, and above this a second concrete volume accommodates the bedrooms.

© Juan Purcell

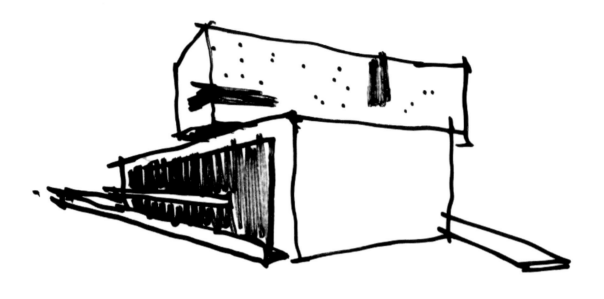

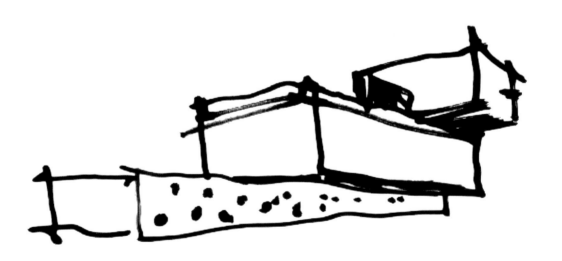

Preliminary sketches

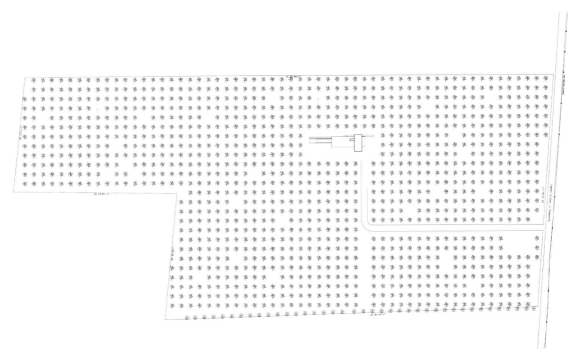

Site plan

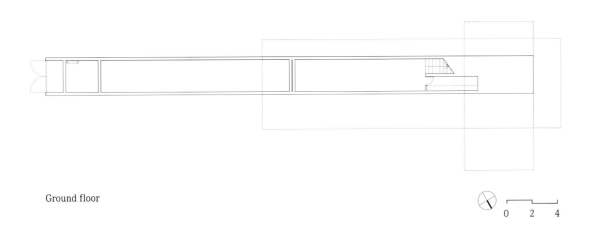

Ground floor

0 2 4

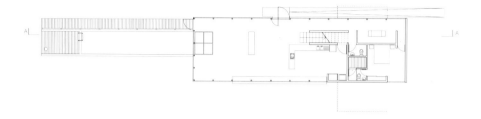

First floor

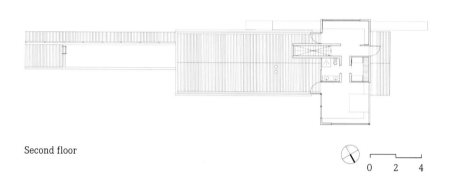

Second floor

0　2　4

Elevations

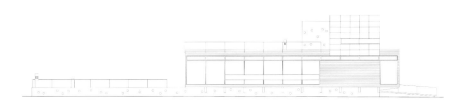

North elevation

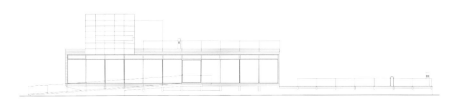

South elevation

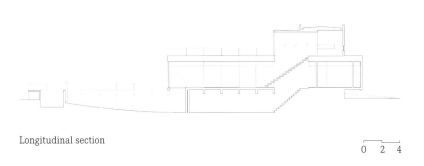

Longitudinal section

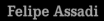

0   2   4

■ Felipe Assadi was born in 1971 and graduated in architecture at the University of Finis Terrae, Santiago in 1996. In that same year he was chosen for the 3rd Design Bienal in Chile, and later took part in a number of exhibitions both nationally and internationally. His work has mainly focused on the design of single-family homes and commercial spaces. He is a columnist in the architecture and interior design newspaper "El Mercurio" and a teacher at the Finis Terrae, Andrés Bello and Diego Portales universities, in Santiago.

Felipe Assadi

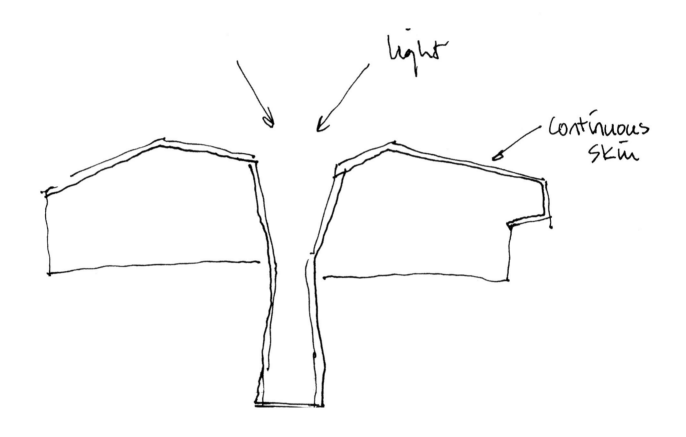

Budget: $ 750,000

■ Two main bodies form the general composition of the project. The first, the ground floor, consists of a volume of natural rock, taken from the area surrounding the site, which adapts perfectly to the area's topography. The second, protruding from on top of the first, is a light body of metal, wood and glass, which bends to capture the best views of the lake and to guarantee the greatest flow of natural light. The house is organised around a central structure, that occupies both floors, but comes into being more on the second where it opens up to house the amenities – like the kitchen, the bathroom, and the chimney – and the air-conditioning systems, leaving the rest of the space free.

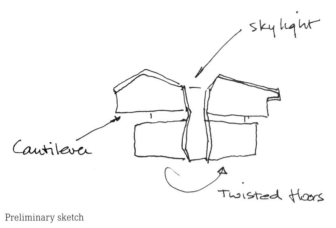

Preliminary sketch

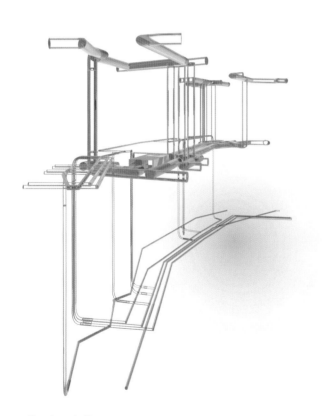

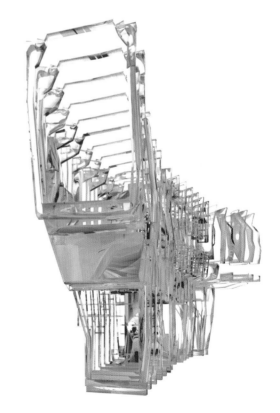

Structure studies

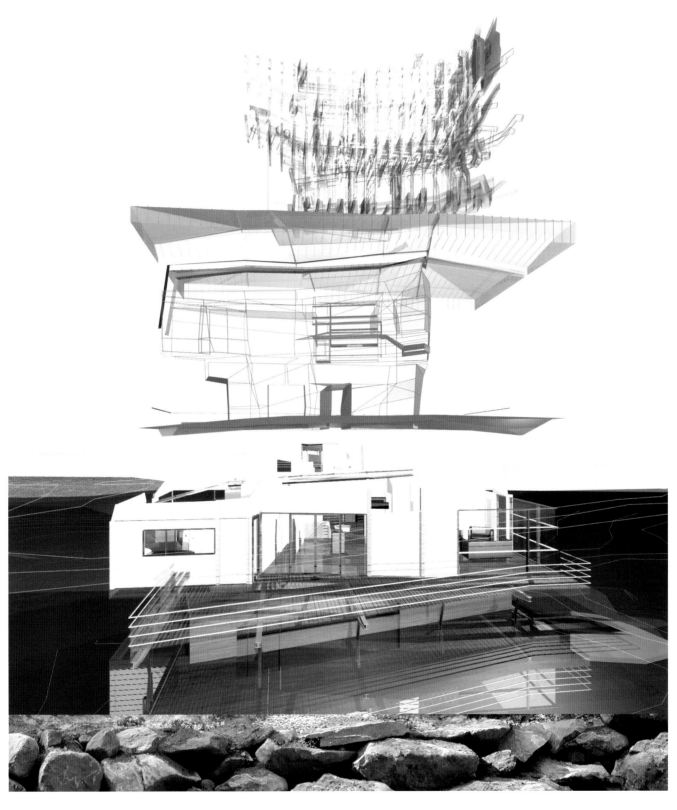

Render

Perspective

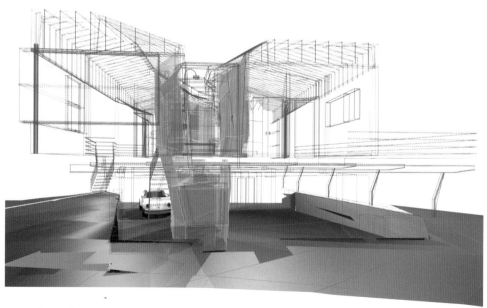

Perspective section

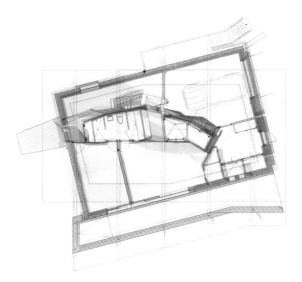

Ground floor

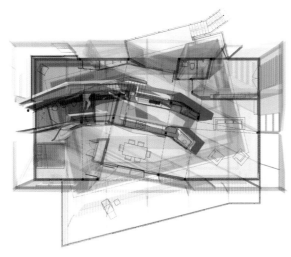

First floor

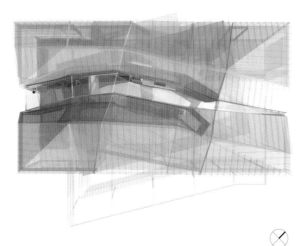

Roof plan

■ Winka Dubbeldam is the founder of Archi-Tectonics, a firm founded in New York in 1994. The studio operates in a traditional way, considering research to be a fundamental part of the design process, and using the latest computer technology as a basic component in the creation process. In this sense, the computer, as well as being a medium for representing ideas, constitutes a tool that generates proposals. The dynamic structures obtained are not simply three-dimensional forms, they are elements that can measure stress, create intelligent systems and organise how it will all work.

Archi-Tectonics

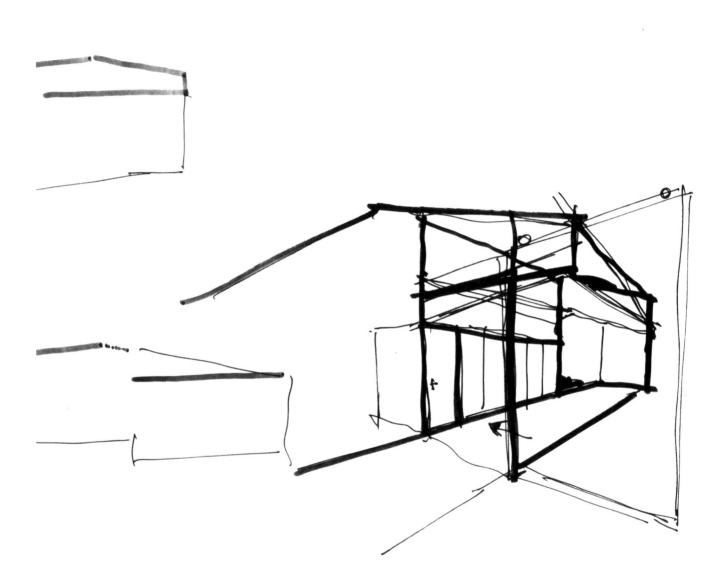

Budget: $ 1,500,000

■ The clients that commissioned this project wanted to live in a single-story house that at the same time stood as a sculptural object with the backdrop of the surrounding housing typology. The angular shape used in the volume accentuates the light slope of the plot and generates a semi-subterranean floor that houses the access and the garage. The exterior form and finish, of concrete panels, appears closed and solid. However an interior courtyard gives light and depth to the inside.

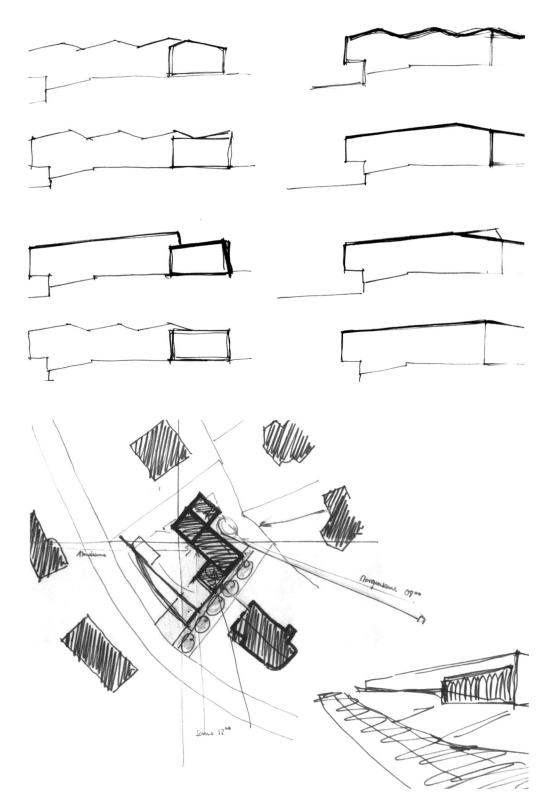

Preliminary sketches

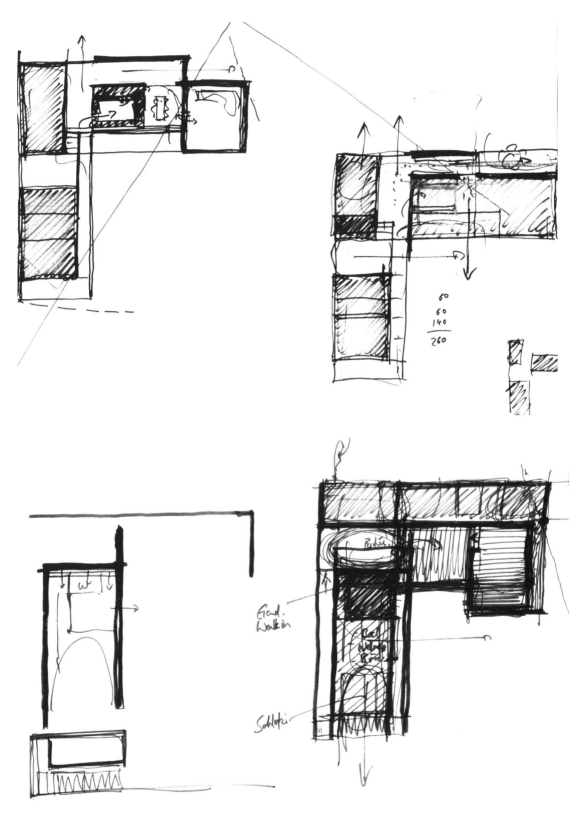

Distribution diagram

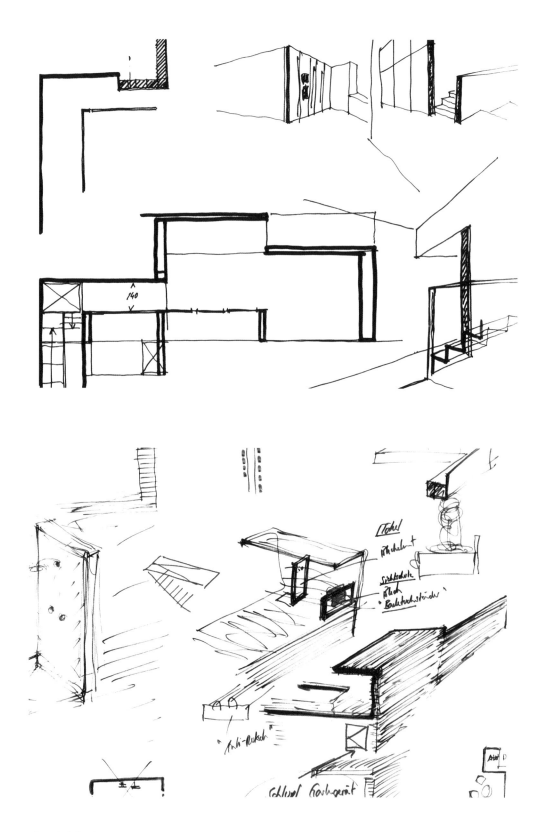

Detailed sketches

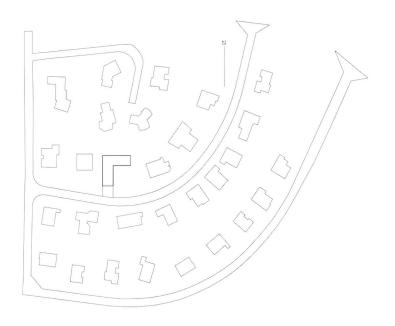

Site plan

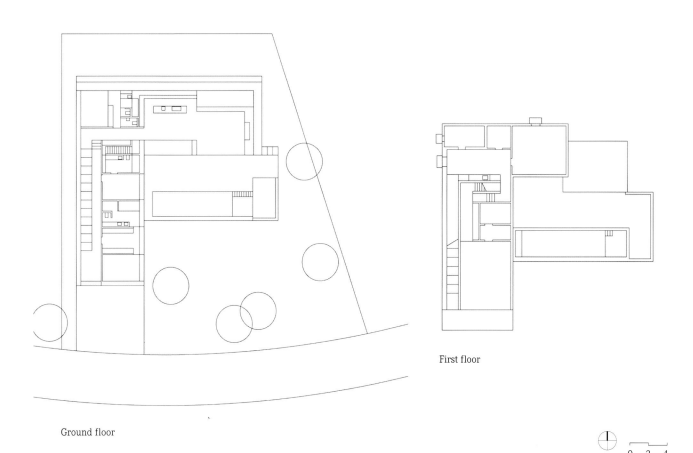

Ground floor

First floor

0 2 4

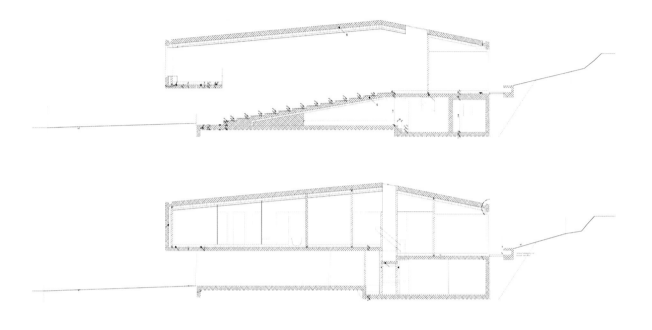

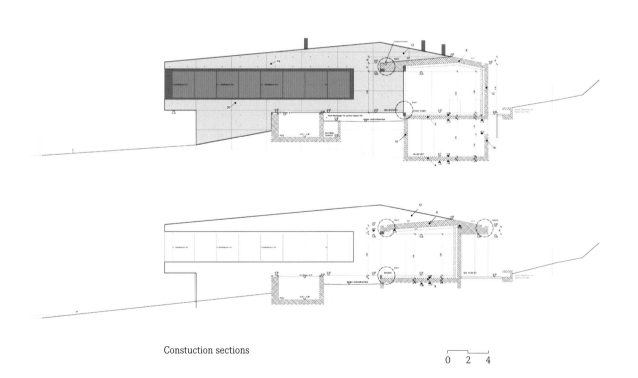

Constuction sections

0   2   4

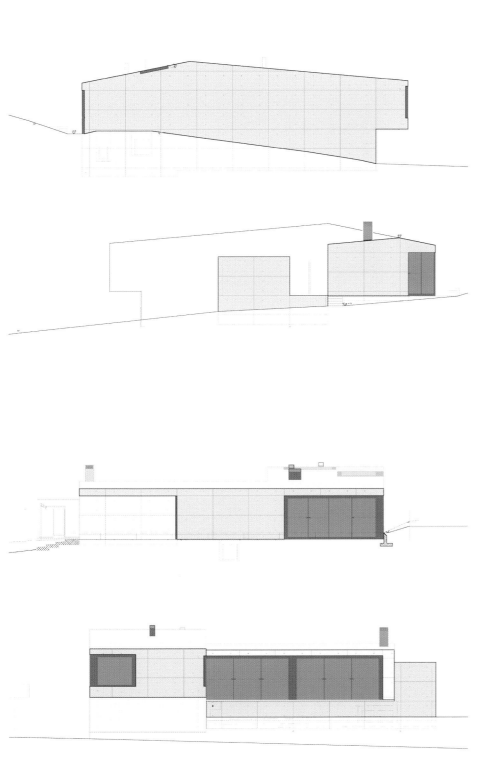

Elevations

Peter Kunz, after graduating in Winterthur in 1987, travelled to United States to complement his studies and carry out some professional work. On his return in 1991, he opened his first studio in Winterthur, and later, in 2002, another in Zürich. His work focuses on residential constructions and commercial, sport-related and institutional buildings.

Peter Kunz Architektur

Jun Aoki **House C** Tokyo, Japan

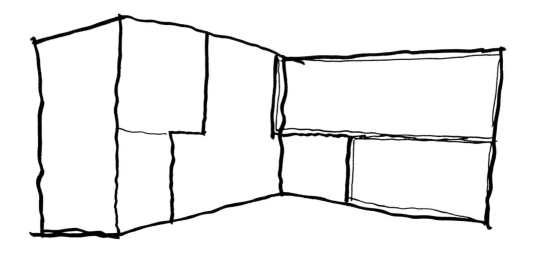

■ This house stands on a square plot and has a rectangular garden positioned in one of the corners. To preserve this, the only exterior space that the house opens to, the building is in the shape of an L that embraces the garden. The exterior cladding, made from steel and copper frames, to achieve minimum width of the various beams, appears sober and austere. In contrast to this, the inside is a collection of small rooms that generate their own character, depending on the materials used: there is a room painted beige, another clad in panels of galvanized sheet metal, another tiled, etcetera.

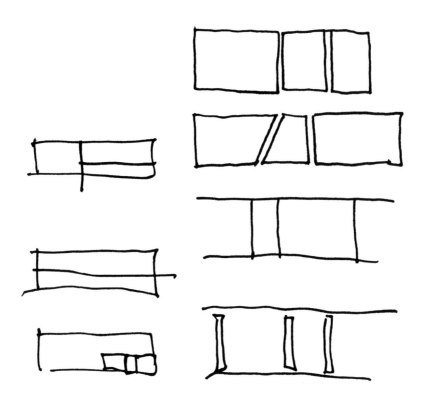

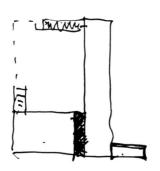

Preliminary sketches

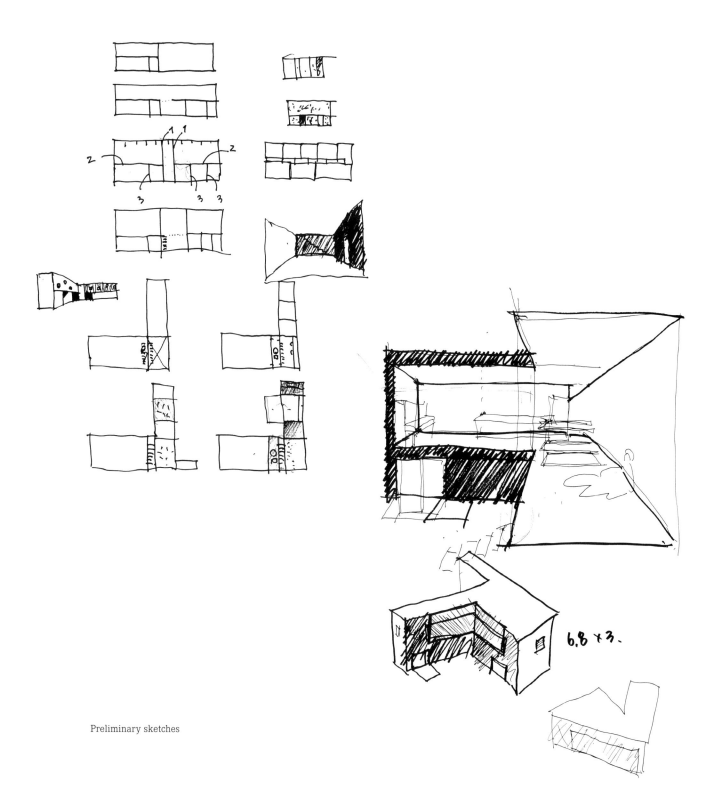

Preliminary sketches

6.8 x 3.

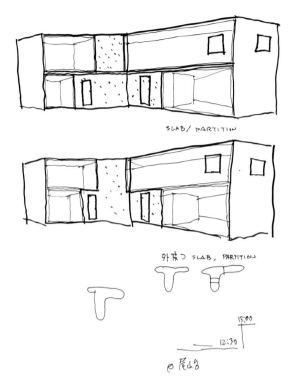

Volumetric study

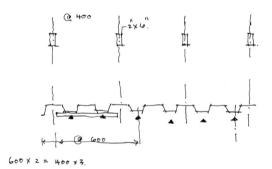

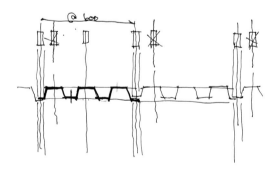

Structure studies

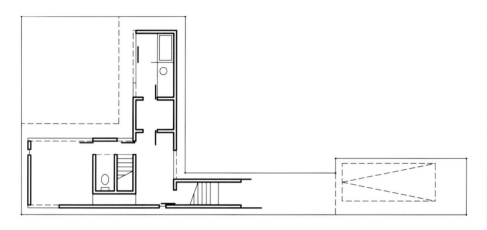

Ground floor

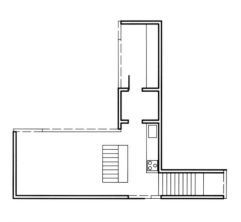

First floor

0   1   2

■ Jun Aoki graduated in architecture at the University of Tokyo and worked in the Arata Isozaki & Associates office before establishing his own firm in the same city in 1991 with the aim, as he put it, of "doing anything that seemed interesting". In this sense, his work is very diverse, encompassing single family houses, civil architecture, and also fashion shops, such as his recent series of projects for Louis Vuitton.

Jun Aoki

Kazuhiko Oishi **City Cube** Sawara-ku, Fukuoka, Japan

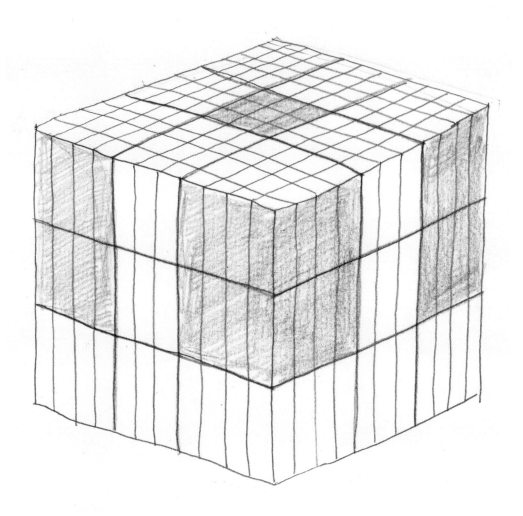

■ This building develops from the typical model of a three-story house and acts as a concise and practical structural system, which attempts to reduce construction costs. The square plan, measuring 31.2 ft across, is divided in three parts, giving way to the segmentation of nine modules per story thereby organising the different rooms of the house in a practical and systematic way. In order to give privacy to the rooms, a concrete platform was built that encloses the rooms and acts as a base to the composition. On the upper part, steel framing forms a light structure, clad in translucid glass panels, which allow the light to pass and lend privacy to the interior.

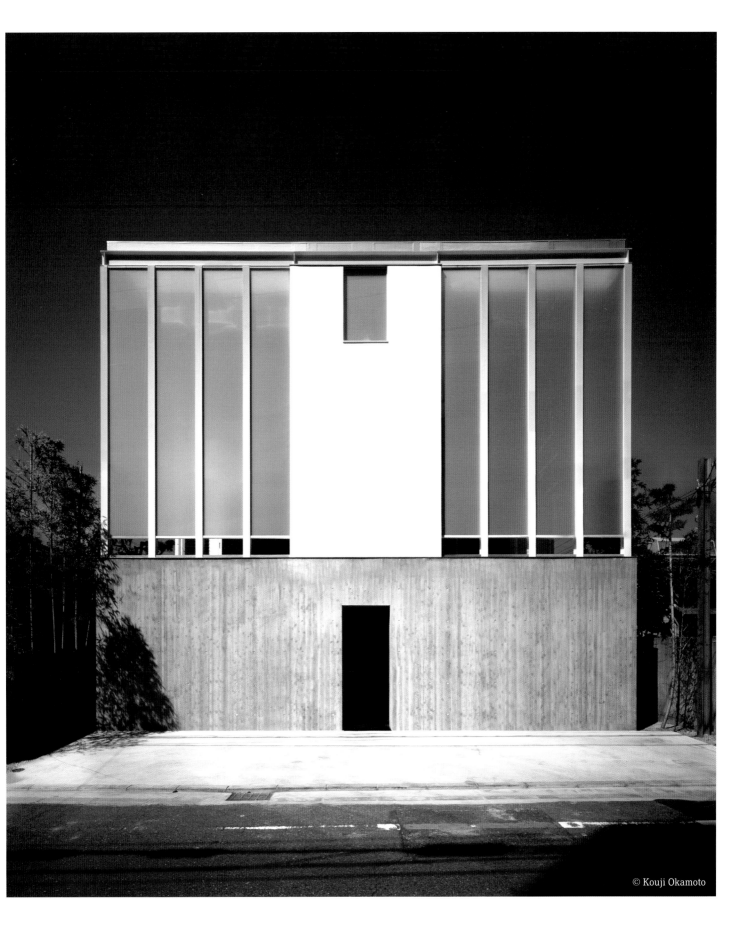

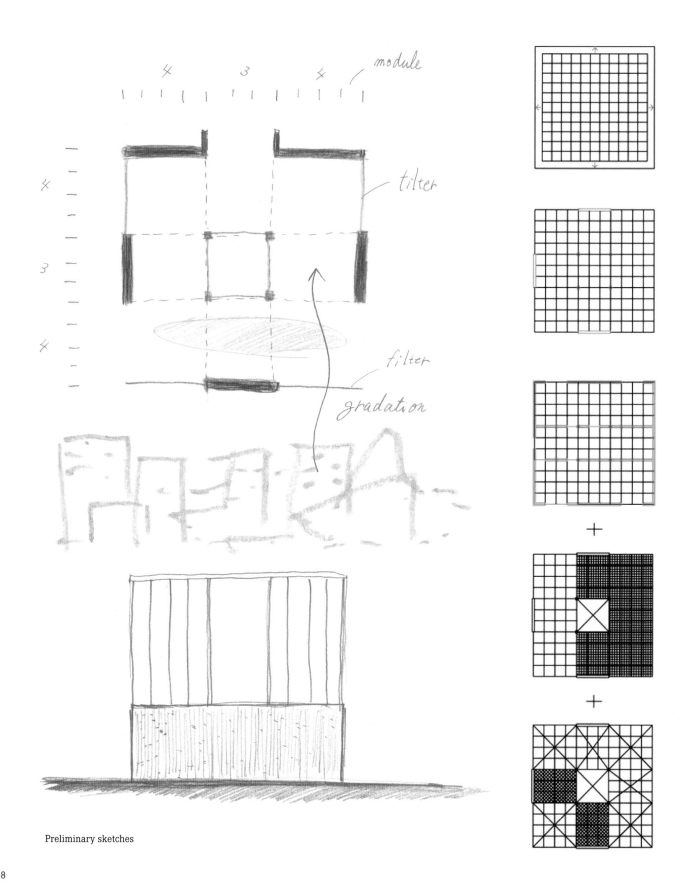

Preliminary sketches

Interior perspectives

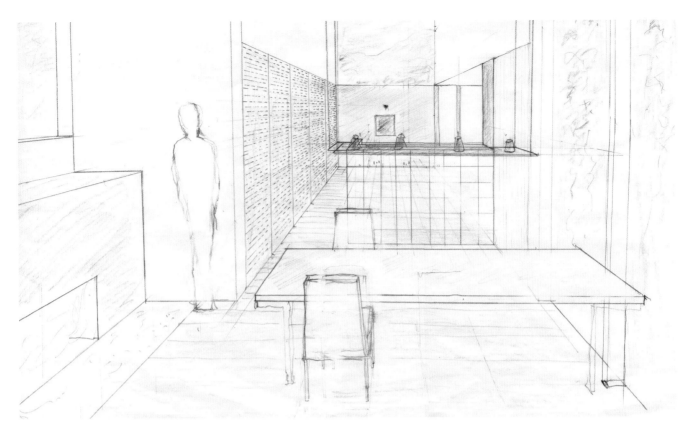

Interior perspective

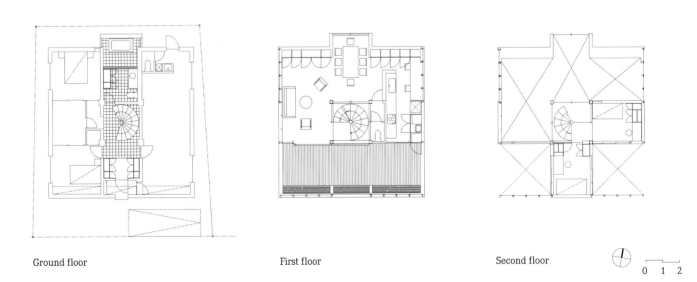

Ground floor

First floor

Second floor

0   1   2

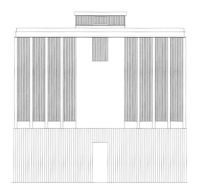

Elevations

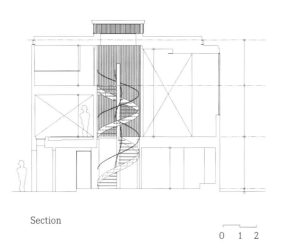

Section

0   1   2

Kazuhiko Oishi was born in Fukuoka in 1956 and graduated in Environmental Design in the Kyushu Design Institute in 1978. After graduating he worked for Mamoru Yamada Architects until 1994. In 1995 he founded his own architectural firm, where his permanent goal is to find the link between a building's inhabitants and the exterior through an "abstract filter of nature". Natural phenomena, like rain, fog, a sunset or a sea breeze are elements that determine the design in all of his work.

Kazuhiko Oishi

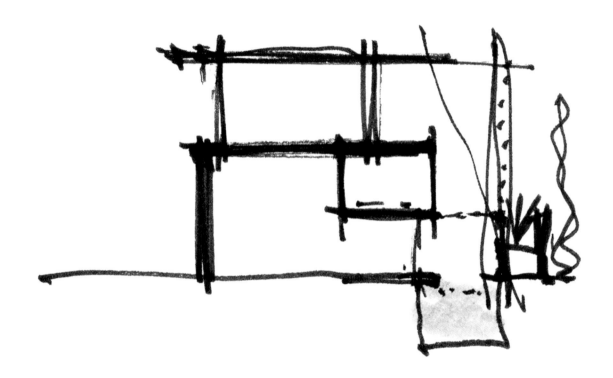

■ The 700 Palms Residence was designed as a flexible building that could accommodate a large family along with their occasional guests. The main challenges of this design consisted of taking full advantage of the combination of volumes and the natural light in order to create an intimate, sensitive environment, which would integrate with the surroundings. Fine and sometimes rustic materials were used, which allow the composition to integrate with its bohemian setting in Venice. The architects also attempted, via multipurpose spaces, to dissolve the barriers between the interior and the exterior. A series of native palms border the site, which soften the visual impact of the three stories, and in turn provide the various outdoor areas with shade.

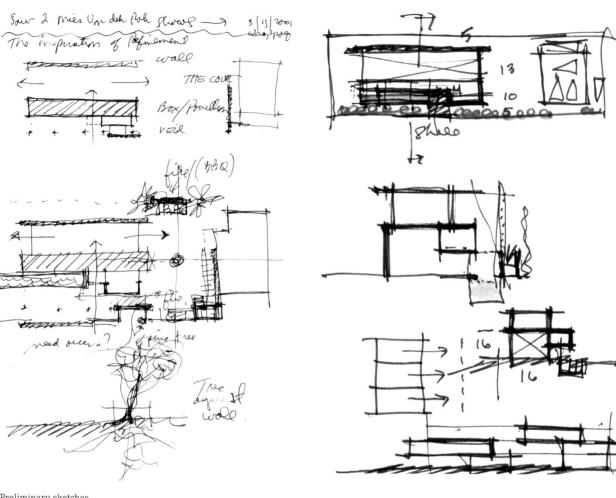

Preliminary sketches

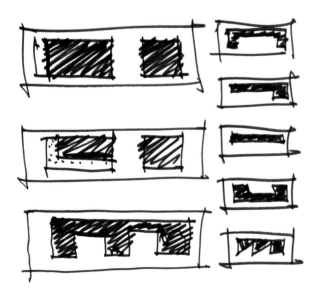

Elevation studies

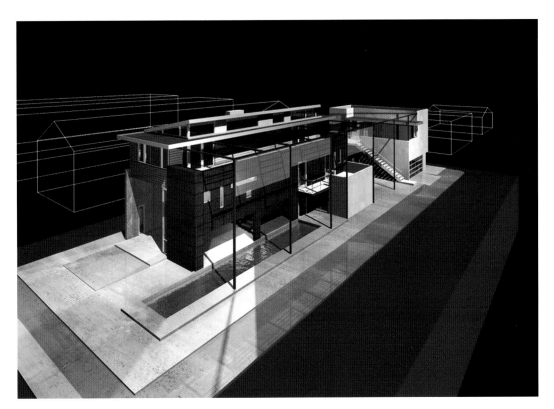

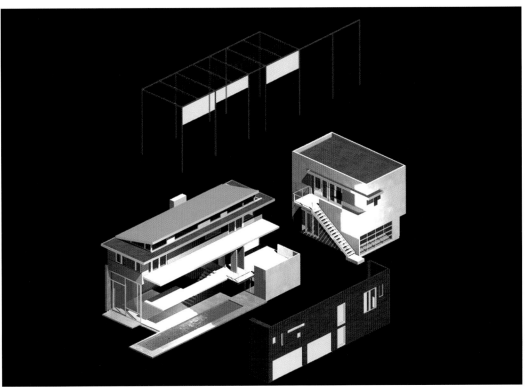

Renders

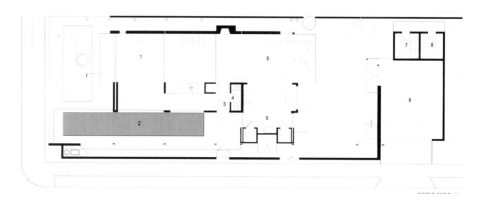

Ground floor

First floor

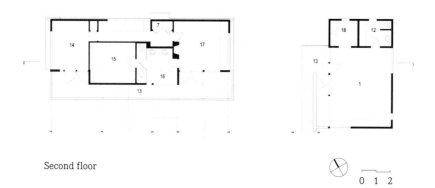

Second floor

0 1 2

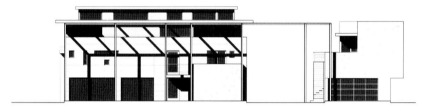

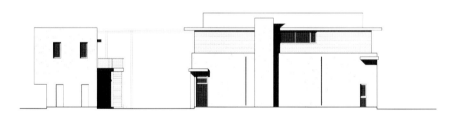

Elevations

Sections

0 1 2

■ After graduating at the Rensselaer Polytechnic Institute, Steven Ehrlich joined the organisation, Peace Corps, where he remained for two years, and during which time, in 1969, he travelled to Marrakech. After spending several years in North Africa, researching, studying and giving classes on the region's architecture, he returned to Los Angeles, where he founded his own architectural firm. His work is characterised by the search for relations between interior and exterior, as well as his interpretation of architecture as a kinetic experience.

Steven Ehrlich
Architects

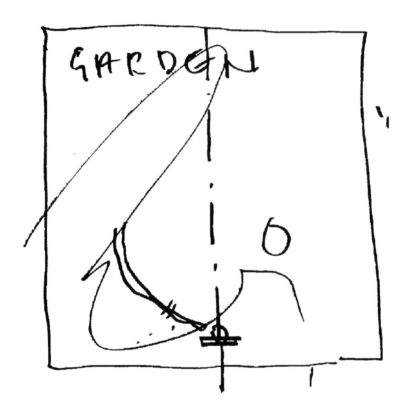

Budget: $ 100,000

■ Danielson House is a small home conceived to be enjoyed for short periods of time. The clients' reduced budget – one a meteorologist and the other a landscape architect – and the peculiar location, determined the design of this project. The result is a light building, which stands discreetly in a rural environment. The distribution revolves around a large, wooden platform running parallel to the line of the sea, on which two differently sized volumes were erected. The smaller one serves as storage, while the other contains the domestic area of the house.

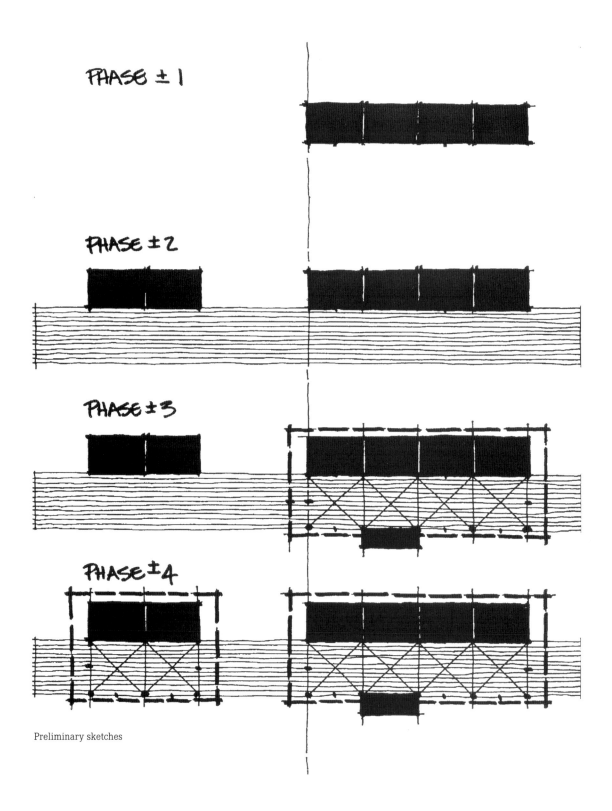

PHASE ± 1

PHASE ± 2

PHASE ± 3

PHASE ± 4

Preliminary sketches

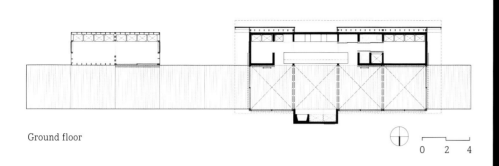

Ground floor

0 2 4

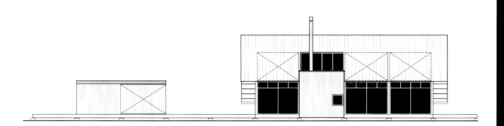

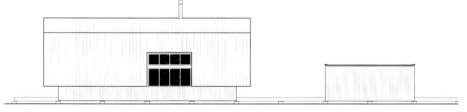

Elevations

Brian MacKay-Lyons was born and grew up in the town of Arcadia, in Nova Scotia. He graduated in architecture at the Technical University of Nova Scotia in 1978, where he was awarded the medal from the Royal Institute of Architecture of Canada. He pursued his studies in China and Japan, before returning to Nova Scotia in 1983 to create his own architectural firm in Halifax. His extensive work has earned him numerous national and international awards.

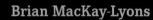

Brian MacKay-Lyons

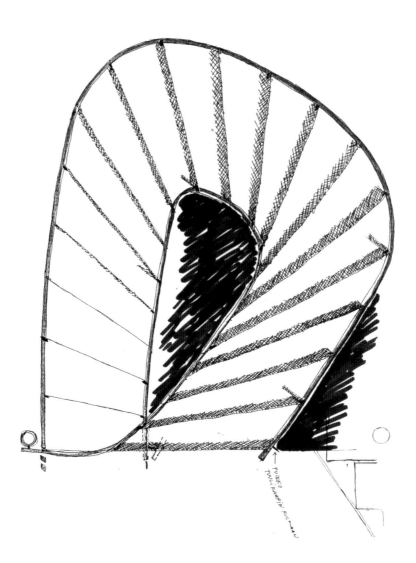

Budget: $ 1,200,000

■ This house was projected at the request of a family of four. A sinuous skin, which takes it shape from organic forms, more specifically, from Moby Dick's famous white whale, covers its 6135.4 sq. ft. surface area. The curves of this animal's colossal body were the inspiration of this composition. A curved wrapping that surrounds part of the structure culminates, at the forest-facing façade, in a large roofed terrace, a metaphor of the animal's jaws. On the other side, glass cladding sets the boundaries of the house, but nevertheless allowing for an interior space, which is closely linked to the surroundings and bathed in natural light.

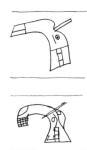
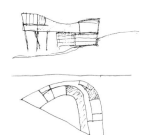
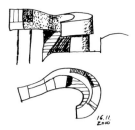
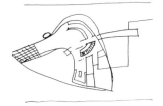
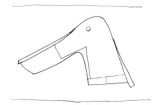

Preliminary sketches

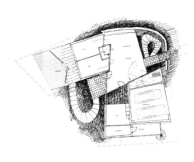

Plan studies

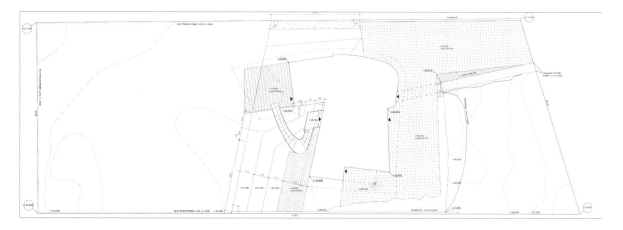

Site plan

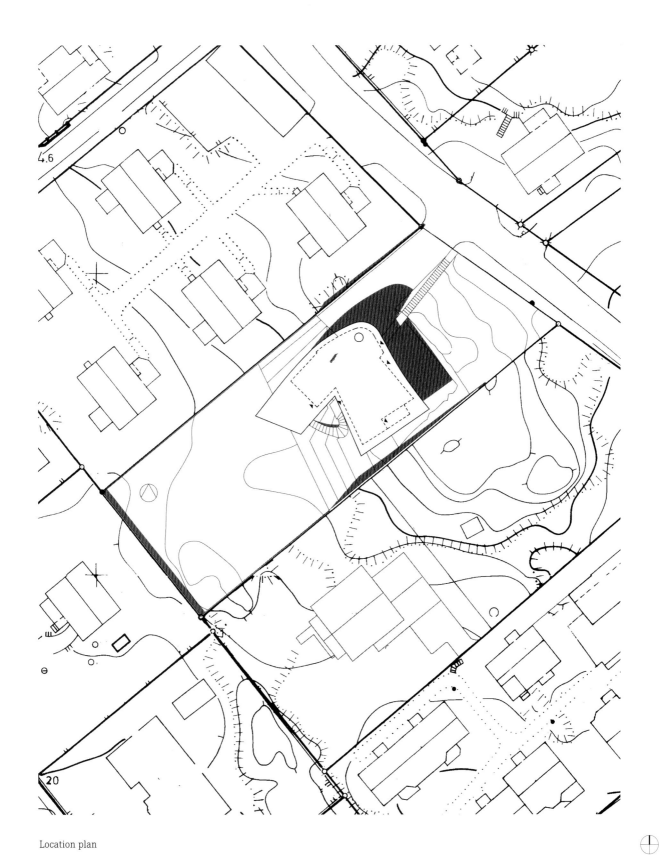

Location plan

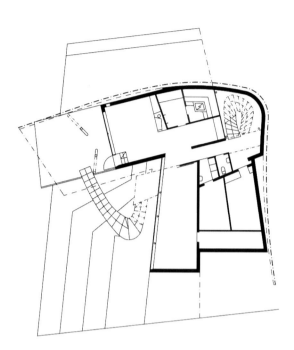

Basement

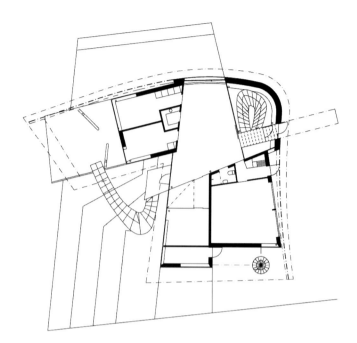

Ground floor

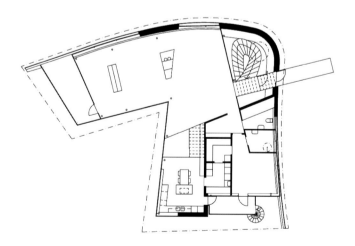

First floor

Northeast elevation

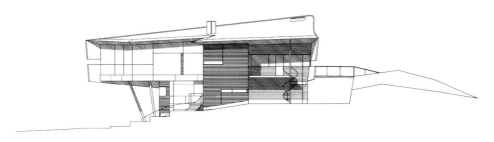

Southeast elevation

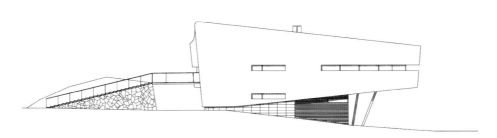

Northwest elevation

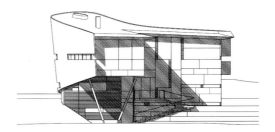

Southwest elevation

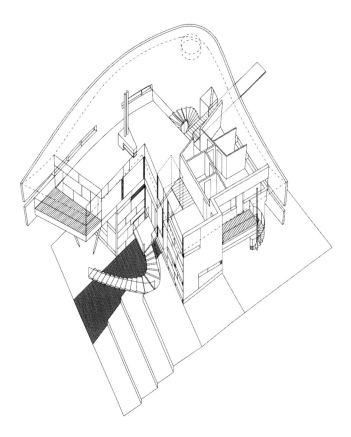

Axonometric view

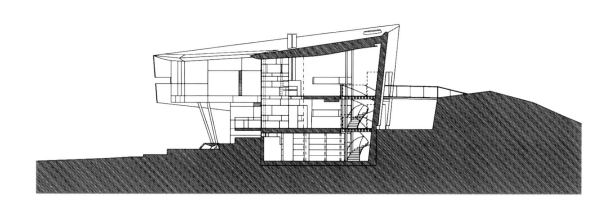

Transversal section

0 1 2

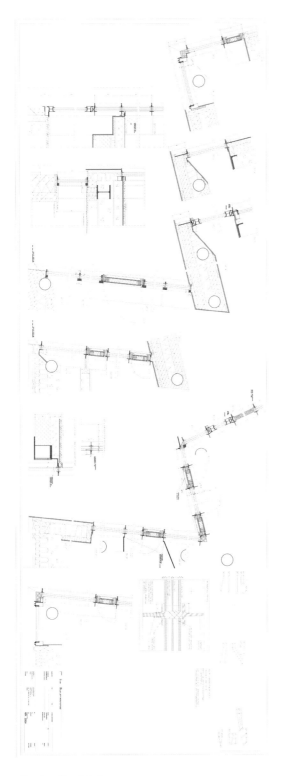

Construction details

Jyrki Tasa was born in Turku, Finland, in 1944, and graduated in architecture at the Technological University of Helsinki in 1973. He is founder and director of the firm Nurmela-Raimoranta-Tasa, also located in Helsinki. He complements his work as an architect with his teaching in several of the country's universities. His work includes various public buildings in his country that have earned many architectural awards.

Nurmela-
Raimoranta-Tasa

RCR Arquitectes **M-Lidia House** Girona, Spain

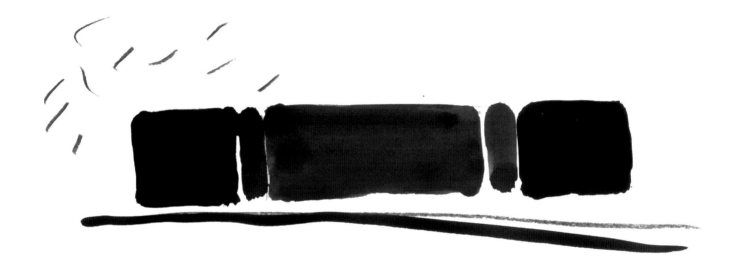

Budget: $ 200,800

■ There are three determining factors in the design of this house: the plot, which is plain with good views, the demands for the programme, which were not particularly strict, and the reduced budget. However, this apparent simplicity is in fact a complex exercise of refinement in design and of optimising in construction. The house was almost entirely built in the workshop and then assembled on the site. It consists of a box with fine walls and large windows, protected by a metal grill, which opens to the outside creating openings, which aid ventilation. The box lies on concrete walls that act as foundations and at the same time house the semi-subterranean garage.

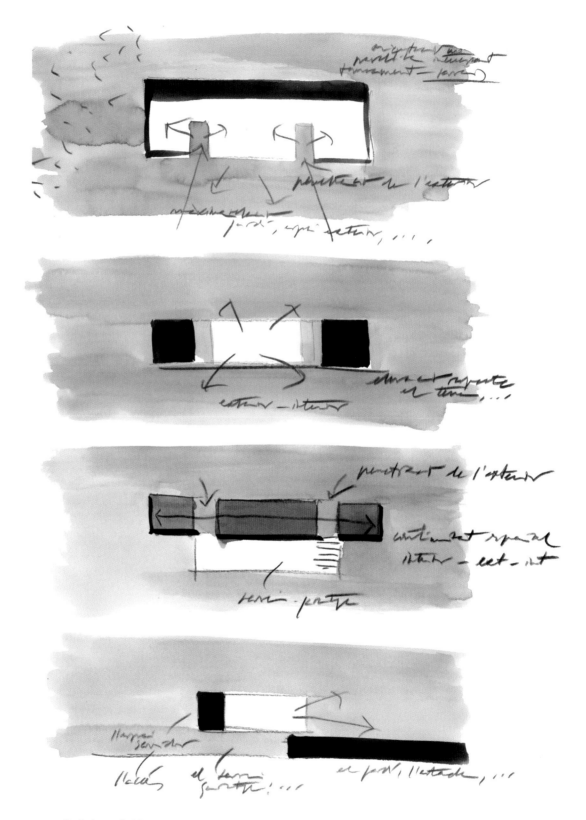

Preliminary sketches

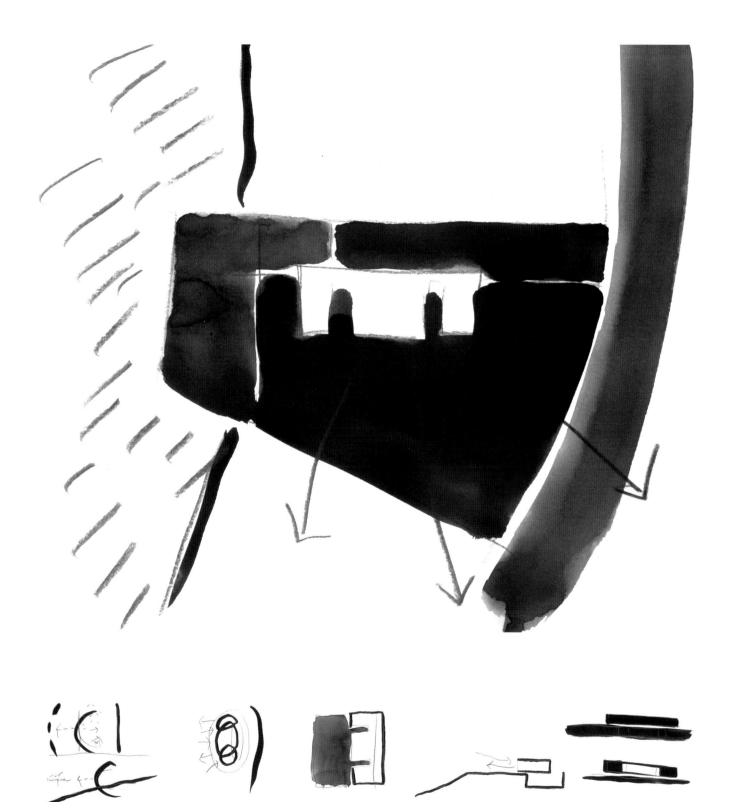

Location studies

Preliminary sketches

Preliminary sketches

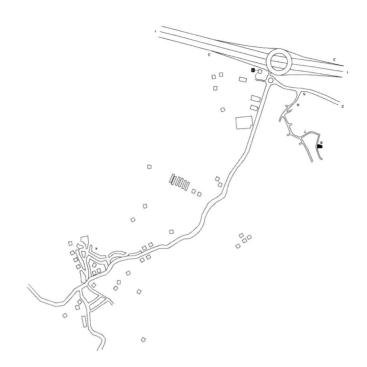

Location Plan

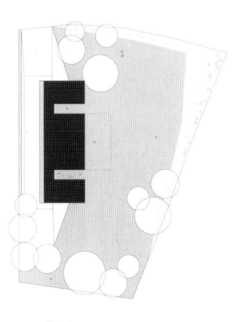

Site plan

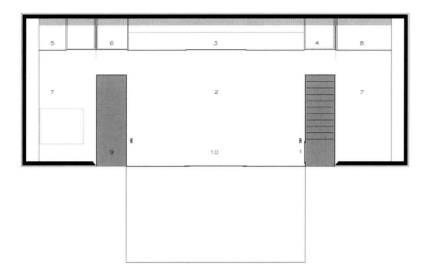

Ground floor

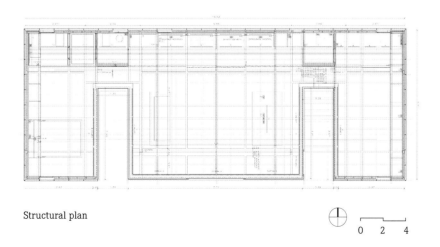

Structural plan

0   2   4

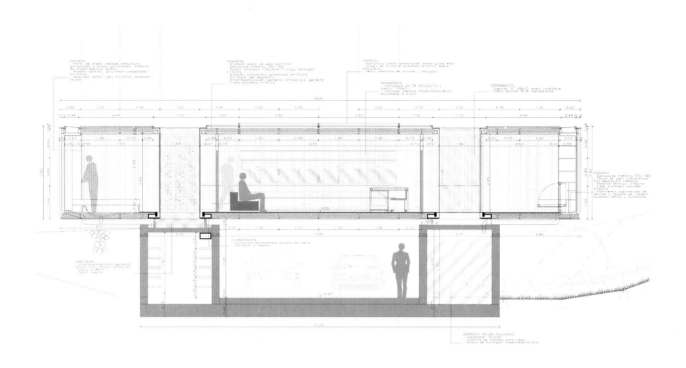

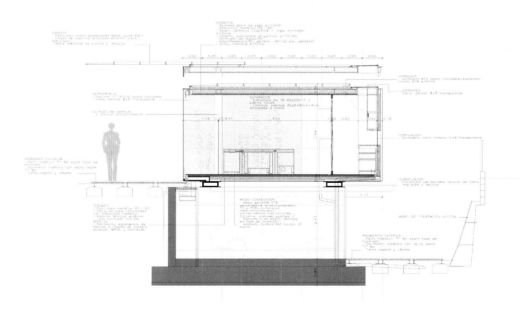

Constuction sections

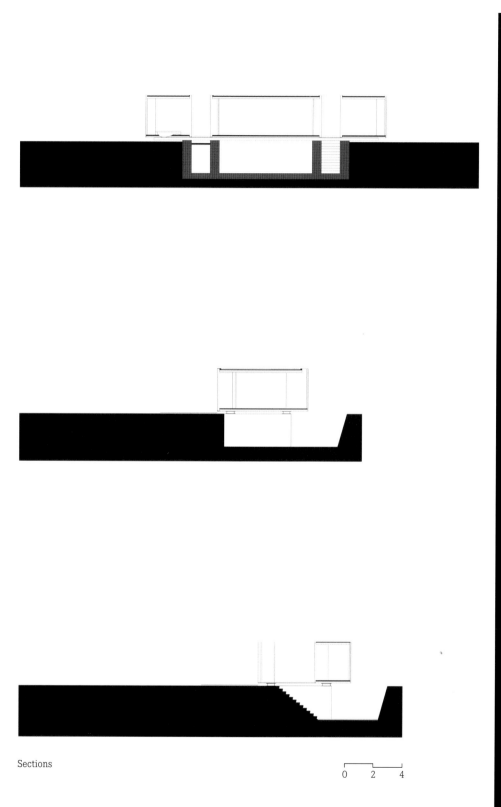

Sections

0 2 4

RCR Arquitectes comprises Rafael Aranda (Olot, Spain, 1961), Carme Pigem (Olot, Spain, 1962) and Ramon Vilalta (Vic, Spain, 1960). Carme Pigem and Ramon Vilalta studied in Olot's School of Fine Arts. Later, together with Rafael Aranda, they graduated in architecture in the Vallès Higher Technical School of Architecture in Barcelona. Since then they have worked together in their Olot-based studio. Although their work is primarily based in this region, they have received prestigious national and international awards, and are an essential point of reference in contemporary Catalan architecture.

RCR Arquitectes

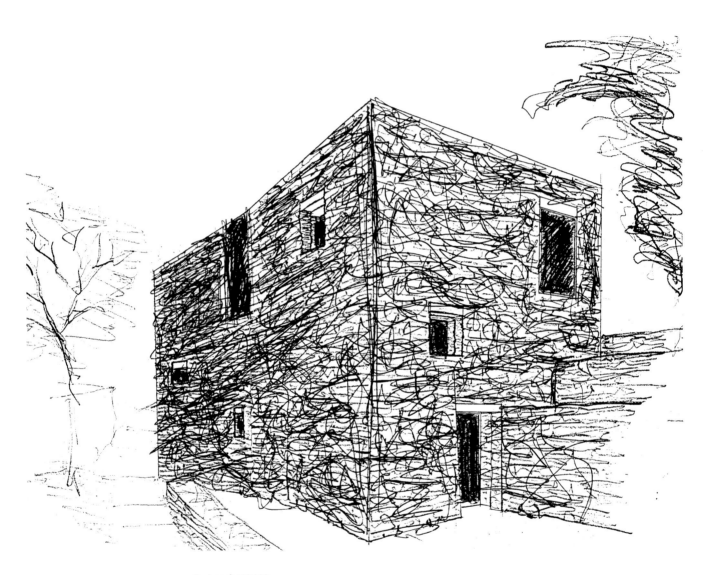

Budget: $ 390,000

■ This holiday home is located on the outskirts of a small historic town and started from an existing construction whose architectural style had to remain in tact. The domestic plan of the building is therefore integrated into the existing surface area via a multi-level composition, connected using small staircases. From the outside the house looks like a dividing wall between the urban and rural zones. Inside, thanks to the combinations of different levels and to the predominant use of wood, the atmosphere is warm and welcoming.

© Hannes Henz

Interior perspective

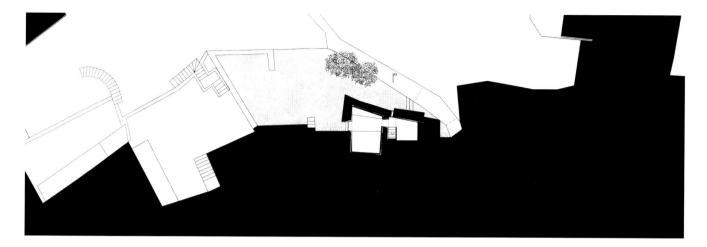

Ground floor

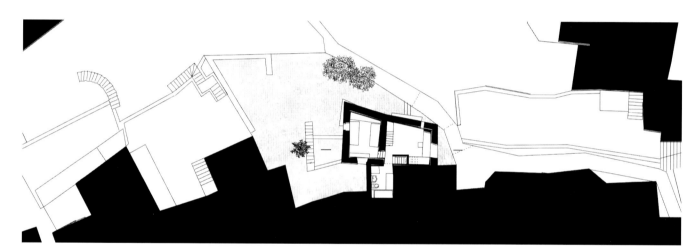

First floor

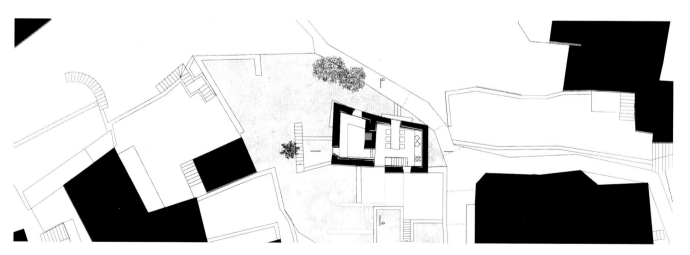

Second floor

0   2   4

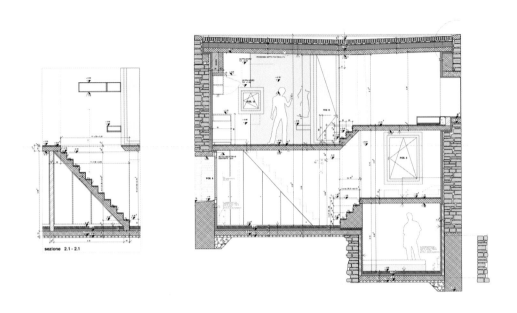

sezione 2.1 - 2.1

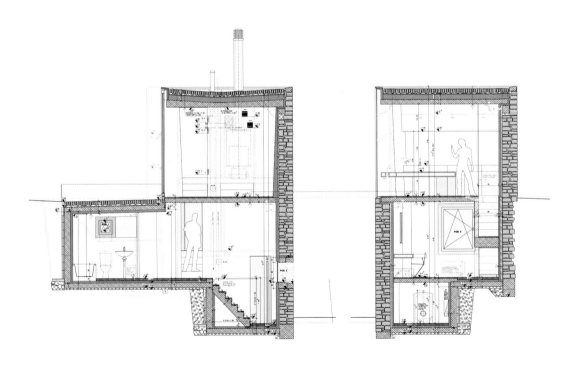

Constuction sections

0   2   4

Transversal sections

0   2   4

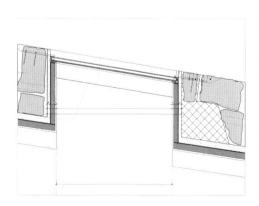

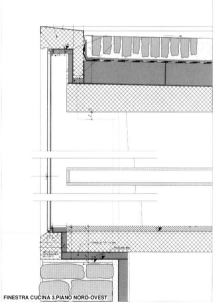

FINESTRA CUCINA 3.PIANO NORD-OVEST

Construction details

■ Markus Wespi was born in 1957, in St. Gallen (Switzerland). He is a self-taught architect and gained professional training by working in various studios between 1975 and 1984, when he founded his own architectural firm, with offices in Caviano and Zúrich. Jérôme de Meuron was born in 1971 in Münsingen (Switzerland). After studying in the Technical School of Burgdorf, from 1993 to 1996, he completed his training in Ghana up until 1997. One year later he began to collaborate with Wespi, until in 2003 they created the firm Markus Wespi Jérôme de Meuron Architects.

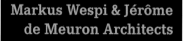

Markus Wespi & Jérôme de Meuron Architects

house weidner, ipsach

2000

Wood

concrete

Lake

Mountain

: m/2d

Budget: $ 850,000

■ The natural surroundings of this construction, next to Lake Biel, afford it exceptional views. The two-story building consists of a prismatic volume that opens completely on one side towards the views. The ground floor accommodates the kitchen, dining room and living room, where the high ceiling opens into a gallery. The sliding windows reaching from the floor to the ceiling provide a close connection with the garden. The bedrooms are upstairs. Their glazed finish is slightly set back in order to generate a balcony that runs the length of the façade.

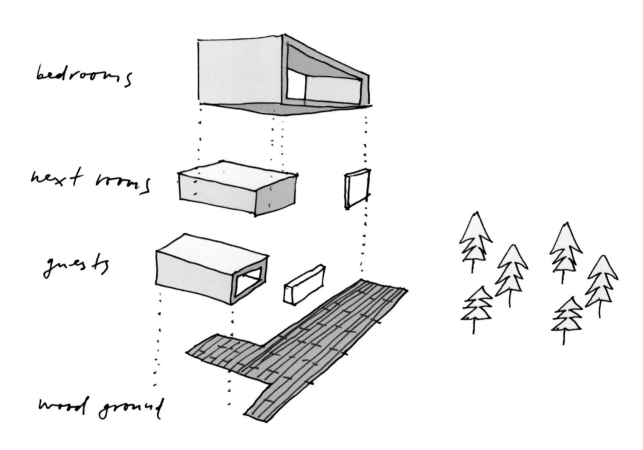

bedrooms

next rooms

guests

wood ground

Volumetric diagram

Models

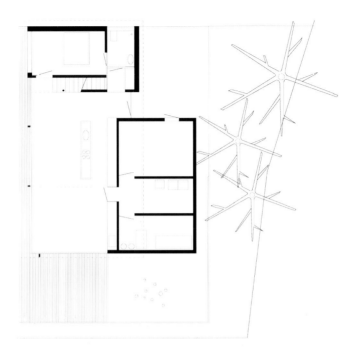

Ground floor

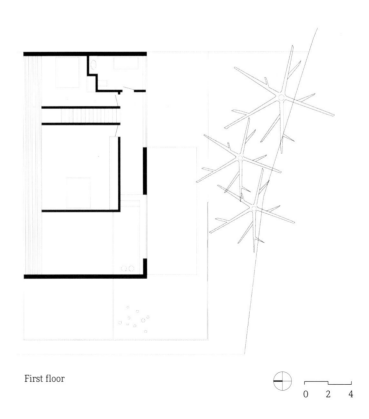

First floor

0   2   4

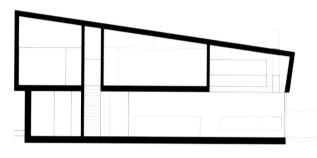

Section

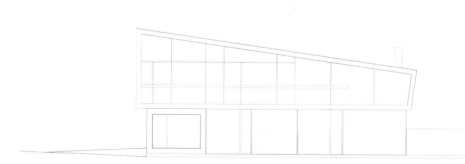

North elevation

■ The architectural firm MLZD was founded in Biel (Switzerland) in 1997 by five associates: Lars Mischkulnig, Daniele Di Giacinto, Claude Marbach, Roman Lehmann and Pat Tanner. Its area of work includes products of urban design, residential and cultural projects as well as the design and development of items of furniture. Recently their projects have received awards in various competitions such as the extension of Bern's Museum of History, planned for 2008.

MLZD